Moose to Moccasins

The Story of Ka Kita Wa Pa No Kwe

Moose to Moccasins

The Story of Ka Kita Wa Pa No Kwe

Madeline Katt Theriault

NATURAL HERITAGE / NATURAL HISTORY INC.

Canadian Cataloguing in Publication Data
Theriault, Madeline, 1908-
    Moose to moccasins

Includes bibliographical references and index.
ISBN 0-920474-69-1

1. Theriault, Madeline, 1908-   . 2. Indians of North America – Canada – Biography. 3. Indians of North America – Canada – Women – Biography.
I. Title.

E78.C2T44   992 971'.00497   C92-093473-0

The publisher gratefully acknowledges the financial assistance of the Canada Council, the Ontario Arts Council and the Government of Ontario through the Ministry of Culture and Communications.

Design: Molly Brass

Printed and bound in Canada by Hignell Printing Limited

Contents

For Bear Island, Lake Temagami, my home

 *Foreword*

MY FIRST MEMORY OF WATCHEGOU (the name given to Madeline by her Grandmother because she peeked into the room before entering it) begins about 1960 when I was fifteen years old. She was my landlady for two years when I attended High School in North Bay, Ontario. At that time her dignity, humour and strength were comforting and stabilizing to four young men away from their homes and the two grandchildren she raised.

It was about ten years later when I became aware of the depth of this woman's knowledge and the story behind her eyes. She came into this world shortly after the time when the fire toboggan (trains) came to n'Daki-Menan (our homelands) in 1906, cutting through the Whitebear Family territories. While her family's lands are about thirty-nine miles by water from the railroad line, it affected all the Teme-Augama Anishnabai. After thousands of years of self-sufficiency and certainty, the white man's expansionism hit our people directly.

The values and certainty of her grandparents and great-grandparent's life on the land were under attack. The strength and beliefs imparted by her family when Watchegou was a child, coupled with her own strong spirit carry her with dignity today as they have throughout her life, a time during which n'Daki-

Menan was plundered by successive administration, drunk with power and blinded by ignorance of us as human beings entitled to the lands we have occupied for thousands of years.

Watchegou's capability to survive the season of the white man and still be willing to share with us a story of her life is testimony to the deep humanness and the principle of sharing and co-existence which in our people are culturally thousands of years old.

Read this and touch the life of a woman, wife, mother, grandmother, great-grandmother and the motherland of the Teme-Augama Anishnabai.

Meegwetch Watchegou

Gary Potts, OGIMA OF THE
TEME-AUGAMA ANISHNABAI, 1992

🐻 *This is my story...*

I REMEMBER THE PINES, the great big white pines, the cedars by the shore. The pine cones on the forest floor, the little clearing for our summer tents. There were no docks, only the canoes drawn up on the shores, no kickers, only the calm of the water, occasionally broken by the steamboat. Everyone paddled then, even the tourists. For some of the Bear Island people of today this may not seem true but it is, I know. I was there - Bear Island, my home, as I remember.

This is my story. This is my story as I remember from my early days, my story for my people and for all those interested in the Indian way of life.

Madeline Katt Theriault
1992

🐻 *An Ojibway beginning...*

DURING THE FIRST HALF OF MY LIFE I lived the Indian way of life, the other half I lived in a city. So, I would say I have lived in both cultures; Indian and white-man's way of life.

I was born at Bear Island in a tent, delivered by a mid-wife, Angele Whitebear, on September 8th, 1908. My mother and myself lived with her grandparents, Angele and Michel Katt. Two years later my mother, Elizabeth, wanted to get married. My great-grandmother suggested that if she wanted to get married, she should leave me with them, the great-grandparents. If not, then she should stay home with me. This was because Great-grandma was afraid the stepfather might be mean to me, as so often happens. So said my great-grandma.

Anyway, my mother decided to marry and she left me with the great-grandparents. I was very happy with them. They were very kind to me and I was well raised in a good home with them.

My great-grandfather died when I was only six or seven years old. But, I do remember him well from several different times and different places. This one particular

Age 3 at Great-grandfather's place, Bear Island.

Great-grandfather Michel Katt Sr. and my mother, Elizabeth, at Bear Island. That's me in the tikinagun or cradleboard.

time that I remember him so well, was at the sugar season. Great-grandma would be busy making birch bark cups for containers to tap maple trees. My great-grandfather would be making trails through the maple bush to tap trees.

First he would load up his toboggan with those birch bark cups, put me in the toboggan too and pull the toboggan. I was happy because I was getting a ride. Great-grandpa would be tapping maple trees as he went along the trail and placing the birch bark cups for the sugar water to drip into. Every day he made his rounds to those maple trees to empty the cups into a large birch bark basket sitting on the toboggan and drawn from tree to tree. When full, he took the sweet water to the camp and boiled it all day long. By evening the sap had boiled down into syrup, maple sugar and brown sugar.

I used to be happy when sugar season came. I guess it was because I would get the wooden spoon to lick and it was delicious! It was the only sweets we had in those days. They always made enough to last us until the next season. But we had to be careful how we used our sugar or we'd go short before the next spring.

When my great-grandfather made a birch bark canoe, I used to watch him. No doubt most times I was in his way, but I did learn just how a birch bark canoe is made, what material was used, how it was gathered and so forth.

For a canoe frame, cedar laths are used to make the framework with cedar strips for the ribs and birch bark to cover the canoe frame. To piece the birch bark or to join the birch bark together, you sew them with spruce tree roots. This root is very strong. Before you use the root, you boil it and peel off the bark, then split it in half. The roots are long like a string and strong to sew with. After you have covered the canoe frame with birch bark, you waterproof the seams with spruce gum. You chip off spruce gum from a spruce tree, melt the gum and paste it into those seams or paste it over the seams. It is very interesting to see a birch bark canoe being made. One can be made fifteen to eighteen feet long, and still be a very light canoe. The idea is to use cedar wood because it is light.

Old Indian Church, Bear Island, Temagami

Mother, Elizabeth Petrant, on a Sunday walk on the ball field at Bear Island. Circa 1918.

We would travel with our canoes over many portages. Paddles, made out of maple wood, are cut down to the size wanted. After being smoothly finished, it is left to dry by hanging on a tree branch. There it swirls day after day until bone dry. This swirling helps it to dry straight.

My great-grandfather has made many things for me from a wee paddle to a little sleigh to play outdoors with. He also made me a little doll papoose cradle. The papoose cradle board was shaped out of cedar wood with the bar across the front made out of maple wood.

My great-grandmother made me a rag doll stuffed with moose hair with wooden buttons for the eyes. She put it in papoose cradle and laced it up. This was a wonderful treat for me to have a papoose doll. I kept it for the longest time.

When I had my own children, I brought them up in a papoose board too. My grandfather made this board for me. He also made a doll papoose cradle for my oldest daughter. For the part that is laced up, I made a beadwork spray of flowers in many colours on it. It was beautiful and everyone liked it.

Anyhow, one day my great-grandfather went to cut wood outside. I decided to go out too. My great-grandmother bundled me up and out I went. I took my little sleigh with me and went up to the top of the little hill and slid down. Here, if I didn't run into great-grandpa's leg! I knew I hurt him and I dashed into the house, crawled under the bed and stayed there quietly. Later Great-grandpa came in. He asked his wife, "Where is the little girl?" Great-grandma replied, "Under the bed. Has something happened?" she asked. "Not really. Just a little accident," said Great-grandpa. Then Great-grandpa called me. "Come on out from that bed, little girl." I never budged, I was so afraid. I was so sure I was going to get a spanking for what I did. I was called a second time. "Come on out. I will not hurt you. I wouldn't hurt my little girl," said Great-grandpa.

Finally I decided to come out. Great-grandpa said, "Sit on my knee, little girl." I did and I knew he loved me. Everything was alright after that.

My great-grandparents used to set fish nets and pick berries during summer. In the fall they used to trap just around the lake, as they both were old. They would take me everywhere. I used to paddle too. I don't know how much help I was, but I did it anyway. They were really my "parents" giving me a loving home with them.

I was around six or seven years old when my great-grandfather died. After that, my grandfather, Michel Jr., took over looking after us, his mother and myself. He was an attractive man with a heavy mass of black curly hair. Great-grandma was a widow for eleven years. I lived with her until I got married, and three years later she died.

For many years, the three of us used to go to our trapping grounds from September to May. Grandpa's headquarters was at Diamond Lake. From there, he covered Maple Mountain, Florence Lake and McPherson Lake. Most times he was at Diamond Lake. My great-grandmother and myself, we trapped just around the lake until the water was frozen. We trapped mink, fox and muskrat. Muskrat is good eating. I used to boil it up and add dumplings. Was it good!! At Diamond Lake we also set fish nets. In October, we would catch a lot of lake trout when spawning and would salt them for our winter use.

🐻 *Making rabbit skin blankets...*

I USED TO SET RABBIT SNARES and save the skins for rabbit-skin blankets. Great-grandma showed me how. A blanket size of 72 inches x 60 inches takes ninety rabbit skins. That is a lot of rabbit to eat, but we ate more than that because we used to make two or three blankets a year. Everyone had one. They were most comfortable with such a warm and soft fur.

You must follow certain steps to make these blankets:

Dry the rabbit skins until you gather about eighty or ninety skins. Then you dampen them all and you cut rabbit skin using a straight edge razor into strips in circle from leg to head, about one inch wide. This gives you a strip from 3 to 4 yards long. Next you would fasten each end in a little stick and you twist or roll it until only the fur side of the strip is showing. It winds up like a string, all you can see is fur around it. You make a wooden frame of the size of the blanket you want and you place one rabbit strip across the frame. Starting from that strip, you loop the next rabbit strip across the frame and keep moving back and forth making interlocking loops. Nothing is tied but the fur fills in the loops. Because of the twisted strips both sides have fur to keep you warm.

My 'parents' showed me how to make a living in the wilderness. I learned to prepare food and how to tan moose hide, how to make strips from rawhide to make the webbing to fill in snow shoes, how to make fish nets, moccasins, mitts, leather jackets and how to prepare bear fat. We did so many things together. They also taught me how to preserve food such as fish, moose, berries of different kinds, and how to make containers out of birch bark – our all purpose containers.

As well, Great-grandma also showed me how to skin the furs off all kinds of animals. By the time I was ten years old I could do everything to make a living off the land and from nature.

🐻 *My elders as teachers...*

THERE IS MUCH STUDYING TO DO about the Indian way of life and their ability to live off land and nature. You have to know how to do things, when to do them and where to do them. Animals are suitable only at a particular time of the year for their furs or for eating. Not all animals are edible either. Some such as fisher, otter, marten, mink, owl, wolves, lynx, weasel and groundhog are not considered edible.

Most of my learning about the Indian way of life came from the daily teaching of my Great-grandma. Some came from the stories and sharings of other elders. When I was around six or seven years old, I remember this particular time. There was an

Mr. and Mrs. Angele and William Pishabo, my great Aunt and Uncle in their wedding picture. Mattawa, circa 1882.

Frank Whitebear and his wife, Annie, framed in their doorway, during a summer gathering at Rabbit Chutes. Circa 1896.

old gentleman by the name of David Missabie living on Bear Island in a birch bark tepee. It is said he lived to be one hundred years old, if not more.

Mr. David Missabie's first wife had two children, Peter and Sophia. His second wife had four girls, known as, Penomen, Sofia, Nezith and Mary-Louise. Only one girl of this family was married. Sofia became Mrs. Harold Guppy of Temagami, Ontario. The first daughter, Sophia, was married to my great-uncle Antoine Katt. Her brother, Peter, was married to Katherine Whitebear of Bear Island.

Anyway, this old man Missabie used to sit beside his tepee with an open fire in front, smoking his clay pipe. We Indian children used to gather around at his open fire and sit beside one another. He would be telling us his life story which was very interesting to hear. This one particular story he told us I have never forgotten.

Moses Missabie, (wearing cap) the grandson of David Missabie, pictured in a late 1890's studio shot. Others unidentified.

Native World War One soldiers in a Bear Island group photo. Front row-Joe Friday, Commanding Officer (unidentified), John Turner Back row-John Katt (my Great-uncle), Charlie Potts (Gary Potts' Great-uncle), Barney Wabi, Charlie Moore.

FACING PAGE *Donald McKenzie, father of Hugh McKenzie, Bear Island artist and friend of the late Ojibway artist, Benjamin Chee Chee. Circa 1914.*

Mr. Missabie told us that when he was a young man he lived where Toronto is today. "When the white man first cleared the land, they found my blazer on a tree, my marks for the trails. They also found some of my wooden traps."

At that time there were no steel traps to be had, so they made their own wooden traps. The crib was made with little poles circled around with the bait tied in the centre. An opening was left

for the animal to get inside this crib and a big log laid across the crib. As the animal pulls the bait the log drops down and crushes the animal. This wooden trap can be made for any size of animal you want. Black bear traps can be made too, but have to be very heavy. "Any kind of fish is good for bait," he would tell us.

Mr. David Missabie left 'Toronto' when he was a young fellow. He worked his way north by canoe. After a few years of travelling he got into Lake Temagami and settled down on Bear Island for his summer home and at Obabika Lake for his hunting ground. He married, raised his family and spent the rest of his time in this area.

It always amazed me to think I actually lived to talk in person to this man who lived and trapped where Toronto is now located. I really believe this is a wonderful, most beautiful memory to have! Knowing an Indian who first lived in the land of Toronto! He was a very pleasant man, very tall and slim. A wonderful man! He was a great medicine man and had cured many sick people and had travelled to so many different homes to cure the sick. He knew so many different kinds of herbs, roots, and barks of different trees, medications for all kinds of illnesses.

I remember another time when we were living at Diamond Lake. My great-uncle, John Katt, was with us, before he went to serve in World War I for three whole years. Anyway, one day my grandfather was splitting firewood outdoors. As he was chopping a block, he missed the wood and split his big toe with the full blade of his axe. The closest neighbour we had for help was twenty-five miles away on foot, the same Missabie family living in Obabika Lake. So John Katt decided to go and get Mr. Missabie. He knew the old man was a great doctor, but he was getting very old and not able to walk much. Anyway we had only one sleigh dog. My great-uncle took the dog and he and the dog pulled the sleigh back with the old man in it.

When they arrived back at our place Missabie went to the back

24

of our yard to cut a young birch sapling. He brought it indoors, peeled the bark off this pole and stewed it. The liquid he used to soak the sore foot and the stewed bark he used as a poultice for the wound. This was repeated every day for a whole week. Shortly after, healing began and before long, Grandpa was able to get around again, thanks to Mr. David Missabie. His work completed the old man was taken back home again by John.

Beginning January, the catfish are spawning in the Obabika River. Every year we used to go to this river to catch these fish at this time. Here we used to stay with the same Missabie family in their big log cabin. They were always kind to us. In two days we would have a big catch and we would freeze the fish in snow. Now we would have fresh fish all winter. At the same time we would gather a lot of fish eggs. Talk about good eating! Another delicacy was the fish liver, a very rich food. But in my memory those eggs and liver were so delicious!!

All of these experiences taught me much about life. It was my elders who were my teachers.

🐻 *A special great-grandmother...*

MY GREAT-GRANDMOTHER KATT WHO RAISED ME, had a very interesting life. Many a times I sat down to listen to her life story. She often spoke about her young days and the kind of life her family had gone through. Her mother and father had sixteen children. Herself, she had fifteen children, including one set of twins. Both girls lived for twenty-five years and both drowned in a lake near Maple Mountain.

Life was often very difficult and there were many tragedies

*Great-grandfather Michel Katt Sr. and Great-grandmother Angele,
Maria Wabi, an older cousin and myself on Temagami Lake, circa
1912.*

among the families. I, myself had three children, a boy and two
girls. My son, Joseph, died in the bush when he was three months
old in March 1933. We were by ourselves, just my husband, sister,
brother and my oldest daughter. We could not get to the doctor
we were so far back in the woods. We took him to Bear Island.
Pishabo made the coffin and we buried our little boy.

My oldest daughter, Dorothy, was twenty years old when she
was a victim of fire. My youngest daughter, Virginia, now in
New Brunswick, is the only one living. She has three children,
two girls and a boy. I now have five grandchildren and seven
great-grandchildren living in various parts of Canada far re-
moved from Bear Island.

Anyway, my great-grandmother's parents, Mr. and Mrs.
Wabie, were the first people to live in the area that became New
Liskeard. They were the first ones to make the clearing at a river
now called 'Wabie River'. The river was named after them. The
Wabie's lived there until the white man came to New Liskeard

Jessie (Katt) Dennis, my great-Aunt in a New Liskeard studio photograph, circa 1920. The Wabi river at New Liskeard is believed to be named after Jessie's great-grandmother's mother, who with her husband settled new Liskeard prior to the arrival of white settlers. They raised 16 children, but were driven away by the growing non-native population. Attempts to reclaim their land proved unsuccessful.

and pushed them off this land. They lost their homes and moved to North Temiskaming to an Indian village there, but they never got a thing for their land. Not one cent.

My great-grandmother was married from Wabie River. As her husband, Michel Katt, was a man from Bear Island they made their home there. For hunting grounds they trapped at Maple Mountain and all through Florence Lake and McPherson Lake.

Anyway I saw some of my great-grandmother's sisters and brothers when they used to come to Bear Island to visit her. Now very few of the younger generation are living.

My great-grandmother taught me much about the Indian way of explaining and interpreting life about them. In the olden days

Indians had their own weather reports. They always watched the sunset and the sunrise to see what kind of a day to expect in the near future. Happenings in nature had meaning. When bees' nests are high up on a tree, it means there will be a heavy winter and high snow. When bees' nests are low on a tree, it means a mild winter and very little snow. When three certain stars in the winter sky seem close together, it means a cold spell in a few days. It is said that the stars are trying to warm one another. When the stars seem farther apart, it means warmer weather.

Indians also had their own calendar. Everything was addressed by nature: January – long month, February – groundhog month, March – crust month, April – break-up month, May – flower month, June – strawberry month, July – raspberry month, August – blackcurrant month, September – crushed leaves month, October – trout month, November – whitefish month and December – midnight prayer month. January is one of the longest months of the year. In February the groundhog comes out. The March snow has crust on top. By April the lakes are opening up and by May flowers are budding. In June strawberries are ripening, in July we find the raspberries and by August the black currants are ready. In September the leaves are crushed when stepped on. By October trout are spawning and in November we find whitefish are spawning. December is the month of prayer for child Jesus born at this time.

Many years ago, before the missionaries came, the Indians' God was nature. They respected all things that God made, the country and everything in it; the sun, the moon, night and day, trees, lakes, rivers and animals of all kind. Animals were killed only when needed and nothing was ever wasted. If so, this was a sin.

Everything was used, nothing wasted. Whatever they had, Indians shared with one another. As well they believed in premonition. When the missionaries came, they told the Indians that this was a devil they worked with. Of course, Indians were left very sad! So the missionaries threw out the Indian religion. That changed the Indians' lives in many ways. They were talked out of premonition which they believed in. It's too bad it happened because they were very clever in their own way and good people.

Before snow would set in, I used to help my great-grandma gather many different kinds of herbs. She used to stock up some in the fall and dry them so that whenever needed they were on hand. She knew so much about medicine for all kinds of illnesses with everything made from nature. I am only sorry I was too young to really take notice of those many different kinds of herbs she used. Great-grandma cured many sick people of all different sicknesses in her days. I know very few, but those I did use worked wonderfully well. It was good for me to have such a wonderful great-grandmother. She helped me set my path in life.

🐻 *Starvation, a constant threat...*

ONE STORY OF STARVATION is one experience I have never forgotten. I would say I was around ten years old. The month of March has a March thaw which we always watched for. We would prepare food ahead of the thaw by stocking up food such as moose, rabbit, partridges, and beaver to have on hand. This one year it came unexpectedly and we were caught without our store of food. What little we had was soon used up. When the thaw comes you cannot go anywhere to hunt. The snow is wet and the lakes are all water slush. No way could you go any- where. Sometimes this thaw could last two to three weeks. Any- way, this time we used up everything we had. I must say that

Myself at age 10 and brother, Donald Petrant, in 1918, at the winter camp at Diamond Lake.

this was the most terrible thing that ever had happened to me. When you are well and want to eat, it is a most terrible feeling to have, worse than sickness.

Anyway, I was walking around out in the yard barely able to walk, I was so hungry. As I passed the old storehouse I saw an animal foot hanging down from the roof where the snow had melted away. I took a pole and yanked it down. It was a lynx which we had killed early in the fall and thrown up there after it was skinned. When the snow was melting down it came uncovered. Anyway I went in the house and got a big knife. I cut the front and back legs off and put them in the oven to roast. When they were cooked, I gave one leg to grandpa and one each to great-grandma and myself. The fourth leg we shared among us. Was it good! Most delicious! This saved us from starving altogether. Mind you, this animal was not considered edible. To us it sure was good though!

The next day it turned cold and Grandpa could walk on the ice. He left right away to go to the Bear Island Hudson Bay Post to get us some groceries. This experience of hunger was one of the hardships that had happened to me that I'll never forget.

We lived twenty-five miles away from the Hudson Bay Post, walking on foot. Bush life was wonderful, but again it was a hard life at times. One thing however, most Indians were very healthy, maybe because the food was always fresh. Animals were killed only when needed and we could drink water anywhere. Our camp was always fresh with fresh balsam branches for our beds and floors in the camp. Such lovely smells from the branches and the air then was pure. We Indians were very happy with what we had with our quality of life.

I remember in later years when my great-grandmother could hardly walk, we just trapped close around our camp. We travelled mostly by canoe before the lake was frozen. One day we were looking over our traps along the shoreline. As we paddled around one of the points in the bay, there was a small deer feeding in the water. I pointed it out to Great-grandma. We watched every time the deer put its head in the water. We paddled closer until we were close enough to shoot. I took aim, shot and the deer fell in the shallow water. I pulled him out and dragged it into the canoe. Believe me, I was happy. It was the first deer I ever killed. We paddled home with our trophy.

As we arrived home, Grandpa was there. I was so excited I could hardly wait to tell him. Grandpa teased, "Was the deer dead before?" My great-grandmother said to me, "Now that you have killed the deer, you skin it yourself, cut up the meat and hang it over the open fire to smoke it. Next you cut the hair off the hide and scrape it, then tan the hide." I did just what she told me to do. When the hide was finished being tanned and smoked, Great-grandma showed me how to cut out moccasins and mitts and how to sew them. I made a nice outfit for Grandpa to wear. He was so proud of my work that he wore the new outfit to go to the Hudson Bay Post.

We have experienced a great deal of bush life. Later when my husband and I were on our own, it came in very handy to know what I was taught to do when in the wilderness. Starvation was always a threat, if you didn't know what to do. With no stores to count on you have to live off the land. It can be a good living. Today perhaps the animals would not be so plentiful nor the water so pure and it would be difficult to live. So many things have changed since many years back.

🐻 *Living in the bush...*

I REMEMBER WHEN I WAS VERY YOUNG. Then Temagami Lake was a most beautiful lake. There were only a few tourist camps with tents. Tents for sleeping quarters, tents for the dining room and a tent for the kitchen. There was only one little motor launch owned by Mr. Orr, the owner of Wabikon Camp. His daughter, Charlotte Orr managed the camp, large enough for 200 people. The lake then was very special with a lot of good fishing. It was so quiet with no noise at all. When the loons called, the water would vibrate. Everyone paddled to get around the lake. The only other boat at that time was the Belle, a large steamboat, operated by Dan O'Connor. The steamer brought both passengers and supplies to Bear Island for the summer. I remember first Captain Marshall, and later Captain Ted Guppy looking after the Belle.

The Hudson Bay Company used to rent canoes to the tourists, as well as tents, Hudson Bay blankets and supplies. Indians used to do the guiding, for the tourists taking trips for two to three weeks travelling through the wilderness. The Indian guides saw that they were safe. I worked for only two weeks and made two dollars at Camp Wabikon. I would have stayed longer, but great-grandma needed me at home to care for her.

In those days there was no school, but Indians were highly educated in their own way of life. They used their own experience to do many different things and knew how to survive and exist in the wilderness. There is so much to learn about bush life. You have to know what game to get at what time of the season and what animals are ready for the season. As well it is

Mr. and Mrs. A. Stevens and Indian Family at Bear Island, circa 1915. Photo taken by David Kerrigan.

Mrs. Charlie Moore, the Hudson Bay Factor's daughter at Temagami in 1896.

necessary to know what animals are good to eat and at what time of the year, what kind of animal furs are good to sell and what time of the season they are good to kill. All those things have to be remembered.

Most things you use are made out of the raw material supplied by nature. Living in the wilderness means nothing is made by factory. Everything is made by handwork and made out of the woods. This is a lot of hard work, but can be a very healthy life. The woods were clean, the lakes and rivers were so clean you could drink water anywhere, not like today. All Indians made a good living in the woods until their lives were changed by the white man. Indians never harmed their country or never wasted any animals. We only killed what we needed in the way of food and we made use of everything. When white man came to hunt, he used poison on animals. Many animals were never found and they died in the woods where no one travels. The animals and birds were pretty well cleaned out and have been scarce ever since.

When we were in the bush we made our own recreation. Some evenings Great-grandma, Grandpa and myself would sit around the table and sing hymns. Other nights we would be playing on the checker board Grandpa made from cedar wood. The black squares were made by rubbing charcoal on the wood. We had home-made games carved out of wood and brush and leather strips. One interesting toy was a 'dancing doll,' made out of wood like a marionette. This jointed doll was on a flat board, that when hit, would cause the doll to step-dance. We enjoyed our evenings, just the three of us, far back in the woods.

All winter, we burned only animal fat for our lamp in the evenings. We had fat oil in a tin dish with a rag wick weighted to the bottom to keep the rag in oil. Then the floating rag would be lit and we would have light.

We received mail twice a year at Christmas and at Easter.

Christmas Day was always a religious day for us. We always had roast of beaver for Christmas dinner stuffed with raisins and flour dough for a dressing. We would have cranberries with baked beans in place of potatoes. That was our Christmas feast.

We were very happy those days. It was a hard life living in the woods but we didn't know any different. At night the log house used to be cold soon after we turned in. The fire was allowed to burn itself out. In the morning Grandpa used to have birch bark on hand to start the fire with lots of dry wood to have a quick fire warm up the house. Every morning in the winter our water pail would have one or two inches of ice which had frozen during the night. We, however, never felt the cold as we all used a rabbit skin blanket, a very warm, very cosy cover no matter what the temperature in the bush. We even used rabbit fur to circle our toilet seats. Living in the bush did have some comforts.

My mother dies...

WHEN I WAS FOURTEEN YEARS OLD, my mother, Elizabeth Petrant, died. She had delivered twin boys and died from their birth. Five children were left behind. The twin boys were placed with their aunt, Maggie Moore at Bear Island while my younger sister and brother came to stay with me and our grandparents. My sister, Lena Petrant, was five years old and my brother, Donald, ten years old. My step-father left for Quebec and got married again.

In September of that year the five of us went in the bush at Grandpa's hunting grounds. He and my brother trapped together. My great-grandmother, my sister and me trapped around the Diamond Lake as usual until the lake froze. During the winter

My mother, Elizabeth Katt Petrant. Circa 1912.

My mother died giving birth to twin brothers, Mike and Joseph, who later died at 9 months of age.

months I set rabbit snares. In the month of May we came out of the bush and spent summer at our village on Bear Island.

I never really spent much time with my real mother, but I always felt I had parents and a family.

🐻 *I became a wife...*

AT THAT TIME AN OBLATE PRIEST, from Amos, Quebec, Father Martel, used to visit our village once a year for three days. He would always come around the middle of June. He could speak Ojibway, in fact it was known that he could speak four other native languages in addition to French and English. Over the years we kept in touch. From the time I was fourteen I knew him, until his death at age 97 a short while ago.

Anyway, one day my great-grandmother had a talk with me. She said, "Grandpa is not a young man any more. It is very hard for him to look after us all. I would suggest you should get married and make a home for yourselves. There is a boy in the village who is an orphan. I am sure he would make a good home for you." When the priest came, my grandparents made the arrangements for us to get married. I did not know the boy in person, but followed their wishes. I was fifteen and he was seventeen. As the priest would be getting on the train at Temagami Station at 9 a.m. to go to Haileybury, our wedding was to be very early in the morning. At six a.m. on June 16th, 1923, a beautiful morning, Alex Mathias and I married with my cousin John Katt and Bessie Turner as witnesses. We had a big wedding and danced from dawn to dusk to fiddle music at Turner's Hotel. I still have a metal dishpan and a cast iron frying pan that were gifts from old man Pishabo and his wife, Lucy. I made a lot of bread on that dishpan.

Myself, age 15, and Lizzie Potts (Tommy Pott's daughter) at our summer kitchen in 1923, the year I was married.

The family of Alex Mathias Sr. at Beaver House (near Kirkland Lake) in the 1930's.

Dorothy Mathias, my first born about one year old. 1931.

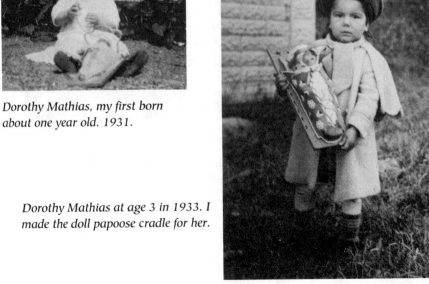

Dorothy Mathias at age 3 in 1933. I made the doll papoose cradle for her.

Alex and I lived happily together, and raised the children, both my sister Lena and brother Donald. During the summers we stayed with our grandparents. All summer Alex guided tourists at Lake Temagami. My sister, brother and I picked a lot of berries, raspberries and blueberries as well as pin cherries to make jams, jellies and preserves for our winter use.

Becoming a wife, meant that there was a good man to help all of us. Alex could make anything. My great-grandmother couldn't have made a better suggestion. Helping one's whole family was important in our way of life, important for all of us.

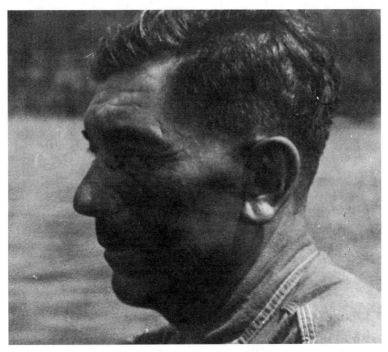

Alex Mathias at Lake Temagami about 1938. He died of tuberculosis at age 34 in 1940.

🐻 *Setting up our hunting camp...*

BY THE BEGINNING OF SEPTEMBER we started to plan what we
should do for the winter. My grandpa suggested that we should
go to his hunting grounds which was north around Maple
Mountain. As was the custom, his father had passed this land on
to him. He said we could have this trapping ground for our use.
He felt it was too much for him at his age to trap so far away;
about 30 miles as the crow flies. We decided to take the offer.
From this time on this area was known as our trapping ground,
Maple Mountain, Diamond Lake, McPherson Lake, Florence
Lake and the west side of Lady Evelyn Lake.

We started to get ready. The first thing we did was to shop.
By now the Hudson Bay Post had changed much of the Indian
way of life. We bought two guns, two canoes, a tent, traps, mink
and beaver traps, an axe, ammunition, Hudson Bay blankets and
groceries. Enough supplies were needed to last us the whole
winter. Such food as flour, rolled oats, corn meal, white beans,
rice, barley, tea, dry fruit, coarse salt to salt fish and matches for
our fires were needed.

We started out by canoe to go to our hunting ground. It
took us two whole weeks to get to our winter camp at
McPherson Lake. On our travel we killed many partridges and
ducks. We set rabbit snares and fish nets and had lots to eat
along the way. It was all fresh food and with our berry preserves
we had enough to make a lovely feast.

We would stop to camp nearly every second portage. We
worked hard as we had to carry everything on our backs. It took
us many trips before we could finish one portage. My brother
and husband were in one canoe and my sister and myself in an-

other. After two weeks, we finally reached our destination to be our new headquarters for the winter.

For the first few mornings we were there, we were sleeping in a tent. One morning my husband got up and went out. He came right back in, grabbed his gun, said to us, "No noise please." As he left, I got up to see what was going on. When I looked out I saw my husband paddling across the McPherson narrows towards a standing moose. Alex shot it and down it went. When he came back for a hunting knife, my sister and brother were both up, so we went with my husband. We pulled the moose out of the water, skinned it and cut it in four quarters. We tied a rope on the moose

Myself, Alex and my sister, Lena, on Island 672, Lake Temagami, with deer carcass on dock and dog called Oski. Circa 1925.

and sank it in the middle of the river. Dry cedar was tied on the rope as a marker for the spot.

Dry cedar floats on the water and meat keeps well in the water because the running water is always cold. Also the meat was protected from the house flies. Every time we needed some meat, we hoisted it up, cut off a piece and sank it back down again. We did this until the meat was used up. We tanned the moose hide and I made mitts and moccasins for each one of us. We had good outfits for the fall.

There was a little log cabin there. We cleaned it out, repaired it some and put our groceries inside. From this spot we went hunting, one week away at a time. We travelled from this, our hunting camp, in a different direction each time.

🐻 *October fishing...*

ONE DAY IN OCTOBER WE TRAVELLED from our hunting camp to Florence Lake to look for fish. When we arrived there, we looked for the signs of lake trout spawning. This is easy to find because the fish clear the bottom of the lake where they gather to spawn. Anyway, we set our fish net and were not even finished setting the net when the fish were already caught. So we just stayed there and went back and forth to take out the fish from the net from 8:00 p.m. to 10:00 in the evening. Finally, I said to my husband, "Enough of this fish business, I am tired." So we unloaded the fish again and went home to our camp. It was a beautiful evening with full moon. Trout always spawn at October full moon.

The next morning I said to my husband, "Before we go to the fish, you get me some moss." He did. He got me two big bags of it and we went to where the fish were to clean them. We took the insides out, cut the heads off and wiped the fish with that moss. It really works. The moss dries the fish very clean.

My husband said to me, "Where are we going to put all these fish? We have nothing to use." I replied, "You get me several sheets of birch bark and I will make baskets to use." While he was peeling the birch bark, I looked around for a spruce tree. I dug up the roots, several yards of them. I boiled these roots, peeled the bark off and split them in half. They make a good strong string for sewing the basket. To waterproof the basket we used spruce gum chipped off a spruce tree, melted and pasted on the seams.

We salted all those fish and put not too many in each basket as the fish are heavy to carry. We took some home with us and the rest we cached away for our return. Each time we made the trip we took some home with us. After we finished salting fish, my husband said, "What are we going to do with those heads?" I answered, "Save them, we need the fish heads for our bait for our traps." Alex said, "I wonder how many fish we caught." I replied, "That's easy to find out." I started counting the fish heads. I counted up to two hundred fish heads.

That October fishing brought a dandy catch. We had enough for the whole winter.

🐻 *Trapping as a way of life...*

WHEN WE FINISHED OUR FISH, we started for our hunting camp. But we set mink traps all along the river as we moved along. We had a good many traps to set. That was a good year for us. By Christmas we had caught forty mink, several muskrats, fox, lynx,

Daughter Dorothy & Bill (Katt) Mathias at Diamond lake north of Bear Island, circa 1940.

fisher and beavers. At that time the trappers and their families would come back to Bear Island to bring back their furs and celebrate Christmas together. At New Year's, all trappers used to come out to sell their furs to the Hudson Bay Company. We made eight hundred dollars for that fall hunt. Of course at that time, in 1923, that was a lot of money. The store manager put on a dance for all Indians at the Hudson Bay store. They served sandwiches and doughnuts, tea or coffee, and we danced till 3 or 4 in the morning. We had so much fun and there was no drinking going on. All we had were violinists and bones to make the chords and we danced mostly square dances. The callers knew so many different calls and they all took turns playing the violin and calling the sets. It was a lot of fun. After New Year's all trappers went back to their own trapping grounds till the next May.

I remember much of the first year we trapped.. On one of our travels to Florence Lake to hunt we came across a black bear swimming across the lake. We ran him close to the shore and my husband shot him. We pulled him out of the water, skinned him and cut off the fat. I cooked it down to make the oil.

My husband asked, "How are we going to keep this oil? We have no containers." Anyway, I went to work and cleaned yards and yards of bear's intestines. I turned them inside out and washed them well in the lake. Next I poured the oil into this bear's intestines. Now I had yards and yards of this bear oil.

The oil is like a Crisco oil. It is very good for many things; fish frying or moose steak and pastry, especially doughnuts. Oil

Leaving Bear Island to go to Diamond Lake by dog team. Circa January, 1932.

At Diamond Lake winter cabin, at age 14.

is good for hair too. To keep the oil I made a big birch bark basket and coiled this intestine from the bottom of the basket around and around until filled to the top. When we needed the oil, we just poured it out, out of the intestine and tied it back up again. We had enough fat for winter.

Every year in the fall, all trappers kill a bear for that purpose, to have oil for the winter. One bear averages around sixty pounds of fat. We always hunt bears before snow as they go into their dens for the winter. After that, you could never find them, the den is so hard to find.

I remember this one time when I was in the woods setting rabbit snares. Next day I went to look over my snares. All of a sudden, I saw a lot of snow and a big bear track on my trail. I tracked it back. Here just where I set one of my snares was the bear in his den. I had walked all over the top of his den with my snowshoes on. After it was quiet, the bear got out and left. What a fright that would have been for me, if he had got out while I was there. Anyway, I went straight home and told Grandpa about it. He went and tracked the bear and killed it.

Trapping and hunting provided us with our necessities of life. Nature was our provider, but we had to work to stay alive.

Dorothy, age 4, and her father, Alex Mathias, at Diamond Lake in 1934.

🐻 *The moonshine tragedy...*

IN 1924, WHILE I WAS STILL NEWLY MARRIED to Alex Mathias, a strange happening took place on Bear Island. Unknown to me, Alex and several of his friends began to act very strangely. In the morning everything would be so quiet, no one could be found.

By mid-afternoon the men would come staggering out of the bush, one by one.

After a few days of this, I began to wonder what was happening back among the trees. I said to my friend, Maria Potts, "Let's go to the bush and see what is going on."

As we walked through the heavy bush we came across a clearing with handmade benches placed in a circle. In the centre was a coal oil stove with a boiler tub on it, ready to boil a brew. Copper piping, wound round and round, led from the boiler to a bottle sitting on the ground. The brew being made was almost pure alcohol.

I said to Maria, "The still must be near here." We looked around and sure enough, I found a big pork barrel sitting under a nearby tree with a foam pouring out over the edge.

I called to Maria, "Come and give me a hand to tip this barrel." Maria replied, "No, no, no. If my husband finds this out, he'll be mad." My answer was, "If you don't tell, he will never know, because I'll never tell."

Anyway, after some persuading, she finally came to give me a hand. As the barrel emptied, the terrible sour smell of yeast and fermented fruit was powerful. All that swollen fruit spilled out, raisins as big as prunes, prunes as big as oranges, bloated peaches and apple rings big as dinner plates with holes in the centre. When the mess was all out on the ground, we rushed home so no one would see us.

Next morning, Alex sat around the kitchen, so quiet and so sad-looking. I said to him, "What is wrong with you? Are you sick, you're so quiet?"

Alex answered, "No. It's just a terrible thing that has happened to my friends and me. We just had a big loss. We'd all chipped in to buy all sorts of dried fruits to make some home brew. We were just about ready to boil it and someone has spilled the barrel. We've lost everything. It cost us a lot too!"

I replied, "That's too bad. What a shame!" And with a straight face, mind you!

Next day my step-father came in crying. I asked, "What has happened now?" I thought someone must have died. But no, that was not the case.

Jim said, "My horse! My horse is dying out in the field. Go and see." I went out and there was this horse lying big as a tent, all blown up. Most horses have long legs, but not this one. All you could see were the hooves. This balloon-horse with foam coming out of his mouth and nostrils was an awful sight.

Many years later Alex died, never knowing what had happened. Maria and I never did tell, and later she died as well.

Several years later I heard that Tom Potts, Maria's husband was in a nursing home in North Bay. One day I went to visit him and said, "Do you remember that horse we had at Bear Island, the only one we ever had?"

"Yes," he replied. "That horse was poisoned from home brew. Someone found our still and emptied our barrel. So the horse ate it. I guess he must have died happy!"

"Well, Tom," I said, "now that both my husband and your wife are dead, I will tell you. I'm the guilty party, responsible for that horse. I spilled that brew. Maria did not want you to know, so we kept it from you and Alex."

Tom just laughed when he heard the whole story. I said, "In doing that I perhaps saved your lives so that you did not die like the horse."

At that time Indians could not buy whiskey or any liquor, so they made their own home brew. After the horse died, they didn't make any more. They were afraid, I guess. Perhaps I did save them.

🐻 My great-grandmother dies...

THIS WAS ANOTHER STRANGE THING THAT HAPPENED during our trapping life. My great-grandmother died in the bush at Diamond Lake. In the bush there is no way of contacting one another if anything happens, no mail, no telegram and no phone calls.

This one time in the month of March, 1926, my Grandpa visited us at our trapping grounds at McPherson Lake, about twenty-six miles north of Diamond Lake. That's travelling on foot. Anyway Grandpa stayed two nights with us and went back again. As he was leaving I asked him to take a parcel for Great-grandma. I had made her a rabbit skin blanket as her own was very old. Grandpa said, "My, my, she will appreciate that very much." As he was saying goodbye, my husband said, "We will see you in two weeks."

The very second morning after his departure, my husband got up early to go trapping. After his breakfast, he says to me, "Get up, all of you. Let us go and see Great-grandma." I replied, "Why, you just told Grandpa you will see him in two weeks." "I know that," said Alex, "but out. I mean it. Let us go and see Great-grandma." I got up and woke up Lena and Donald, had breakfast, bundled up my sister and away we went on our way, bright and early in the morning just dawned.

We arrived at Grandpa's home around ten that morning. He met us at the door to tell us the news, saying that Great-grandma had been very sick. He had stayed up all night with her. I went close to her, but she didn't know me at all.

Grandpa said, "I wish I could have my sister here. I believe she should see her mother. No telling what could happen." My husband replied to Grandpa and said, "I will go and get your sister. But you give me your dogs. My dogs have travelled a long way already." Alex left at 11:00 a.m. for Jessie Dennis, just north of Bear Island. He said "I shall be back by eleven o'clock tonight." Sure enough, he arrived back with Jessie that evening. That was another twenty-six miles he had travelled out and then returned. Altogether he had covered seventy-eight miles on snowshoes in sixteen hours with a two hour stop, a total of fourteen hours on the trail. Alex was a great man to walk and had much determination.

With her family around her, Great-grandma died the next day. She was in her eighty-seventh year. This gathering was always a mystery to me as we were all so far apart and yet able to get together so quickly and be all at Great-grandma's bedside at her last breath. She was only sick fifty-four hours and we were all there when she died. It was so amazing. Now if that wasn't premonition to us all, then I will never know.

Great-grandmother, Angele Katt, with her son, John Katt, in his W.W.I. Uniform. Bear Island, 1919.

By the way, Great-grandma never did see the rabbit-skin blanket I made for her, for she was too sick. We took the body by dog team to Bear Island to bury her.

For winter burial, a big fire was built over the frozen ground. In about two to three hours, this ground would be ready for digging. Alex Paul, a local person, appointed by the priest to conduct services if the priest was not available, came to lead the burial. Great-grandma was a very fine person. She had done a lot of good in this world and had helped many people in her days. After the funeral, we all went back to our trapping grounds.

🐻 Moose to moccasins...

ONE MARCH DAY AT OUR WINTER CAMP, my husband decided to go moose hunting. He left very early in the morning and went to Maple Mountain area. When he used to go hunting, he always was home by 4 or 5 in the afternoon, not much later. This time he did not come home at that time. Six o'clock, seven o'clock and still he was not home. I was beginning to worry by eight o'clock. Nine o'clock and finally he arrived. As he came in, the first thing he said was, "I am sorry I am late. We have to move tomorrow." I replied, "Why?" "Well, I shot down seven moose. That is what kept me late," said Alex. "I had to clean those seven moose, remove the insides and bury them under the snow. I used my snowshoes as a shovel to cover all those moose so they would not freeze before we skinned them."

Next morning we started early. We took our blankets, a few groceries and a cooking outfit. We arrived where the moose were killed. First thing we did is to put up our camp. We looked for a cut rock and set a lean-to against the rock and made a fire so the heat would throw back into our lean-to. We piled a lot of brush branches on the floor to make a good bed.

The next day we started work on those moose. We uncovered one, skinned it and carved the whole moose. Next my husband built a long rack over a fire. My brother, Donald, peeled all the bark off of the poles for the rack. The poles are peeled so that the bark taste will not be on the meat. When the rack was finished, my sister, Lena, had the job of laying the meat on the rack to dry. Every once in a while, she had to turn them over to dry on both sides.

Believe me, this was a lot of carving, cutting up seven moose, altogether about four thousand pounds of meat to cut. We cut all that meat on the snow-covered ground. It certainly was a cold job too, cold on the hands, but we kept my sister busy laying down the sliced meat. Altogether it took five weeks to dry all that meat.

While the meat was being cured, we had the loveliest feast, eating seven moose livers. Once in a while we would throw a moose leg on the fire to bake. When done, we would break the bone to remove the delicious marrow inside. We ate all the kidneys, the moose tongue and the nose. For the nose, we would burn the hair off first and then boil it. It is just like pig's feet, so very tasty. Nothing was wasted on those moose. The only thing we did not eat was the brains, but these were not wasted as you will see.

Anyway, after we had dried all the meat from the seven moose, we packed it all in a seventy-five pound potato bag. It just fit, all of it, and was not very heavy either. We had enough meat for the whole summer and we shared a lot with our friends too. It was a lot of work to do this, but we enjoyed the work, and seeing what we had accomplished. Also it was good eating.

I am pleased to have some samples of the traditional leather and bead work that I learned from my elders. We used to make all our own clothes.

The moose brain we used for tanning the moose hide. We spread it all over the hide after all the hair was cut off and scraped away. The hide was left to stand for a while to let the brains soak well into the skin. Next we dipped it all in a soap water solution for three or four days.

After that you take the hide out and drain all the water out as much as possible and dry it. But you must work on it the whole time. A whole day is needed for drying. You don't leave the hide too long because it will get too dry on you and will get hard again. You work on it by stretching it back and forth until it stops stretching. That is when it is dry. If the hide is still hard here and there in some places, you repeat that treatment over. Sometimes it takes three or four times to do it over. We tanned all the seven moose hides!

When it is finished being tanned, the hide is pure white. That is the natural colour. Next you fold the hide in half and sew it all around, but leave an opening to fit over a pail. Hang it up and place it over the pail and make a smudge out of rotten wood. It must be wood of a poplar tree because this tree has no gum. As the hide hangs over the pail you smoke it with the smudge for two to three hours, then turn the hide inside out and smoke it again until golden brown. Smoking the hide keeps it from getting hard again when moccasins get wet or any other thing. The leather smells so nice afterwards.

Moose hide is the best to do bead work on, so nice and soft. This kind of tanning work I am afraid is a lost art altogether. I don't think there is anyone left that could tan moose or a deer hide from scratch. Although the bead work on leather is coming back, they use all factory tanned hides. As well, the work they do is not all handwork. Moccasins, mitts and jackets are made, but most are machine sewn. Now even the Indians' handwork is not the same as it used to be. It is a pity so much has been lost in

Indian way of living. Even Indian language is almost lost, like everything else.

As I was saying, one moose hide makes ten to twelve pairs of moccasins, depending on the sizes you make. Even though tanning moose hide was hard work, I did a lot of leather tanning myself, nothing was factory-made in the old Indian way of life.

I have also done a lot of bead work myself, bead work for moccasins, mitts, beaded bags, jackets, vests and cushions. I would take them to the Hudson Bay Post as trade-ins. I never got money for my work. The trade-in was for food, beads, and dry goods. For full-beaded moccasins, I would get at least $3.00 a pair trade-in for the large size, and .75 cents for little ones. That certainly doesn't match up with the prices today.

But in later years, when my husband was a guide, the trade-ins stopped. . One day some tourists told him, "We don't like buying moccasins from the Hudson Bay Company. We would like to buy them direct from the Indians. Why doesn't your wife hold the Indian work or articles until tourist season." From then on, I kept my Indian articles to sell only at tourist season and they gave a good price, and cash too.

Not long after that, about 1928, a Department of Lands and Forests' law was passed stating that if any Indian killed a moose at any time, he would be sentenced to thirty days in jail. Well, no one wanted to go to jail, so all Indians stopped killing moose. Not only did we lose a source of food, we had no more material or moose hide to work on. As well we could no longer show the younger generation how to tan hide or how to make moccasins or do bead work of any kind. This law caused much of the loss of Indian work.

Also Indians were stopped from cutting down wood by law. That stopped all our birch bark work. Indians had depended on birch bark for so many things, such as baskets, canoes, and covers to protect things from being wet. Birch bark sheets were good for table covers, tepees and for a roof in place of shingles. Indians used birch bark to wrap around limbs if they were broken instead of casts. Birch bark was always a big demand for the Indian. It also was good to carve meats or clean fish on. It kept the food clean.

It's a shame so many types of Indian handwork are now lost to us, such things as making a canoe and making snowshoes by hand. Sleighs, toboggans, rabbit skin blankets, and rawhide to cut bibeche, the narrow strips to make the webbing for snowshoes, were so important to our Indian generation at one time. The art was handed down from generation to generation. The young learned from their elders. Today the making of moccasins by hand from moose hide is a lost art. What a pity!

🐻 *Seasons and traditional customs...*

AWAY BACK, MANY YEARS AGO while living together during the summer, if someone was to kill a moose, all the Indians in the village would move to that place. They would share the moose with one another until it was all eaten up. If someone else killed another moose elsewhere, they would all move to the new location.

While people gathered together, the men made birch bark canoes. Women would set fish nets and pick blueberries, while the children joined in the picking. Everyone was happy and had lots to eat. Women helped one another to tan moose hide and make moccasins for all. My great-grandmother often mentioned how wonderful it was to see Indians help one another and share everything with one another. "It was just one big happy family,"

*Dorothy, about 3 years old, with snowshoes at
Diamond Lake, 1933.*

said Great-grandma. There was no worrying of any kind, but
people knew how to work and live off land and nature. They
were so close to nature and a lot of love. Nature was their God.

All children learned to work at a very young age. They
worked with their parents and learned how to live in the wilderness. The children's play was that they would do everything that
their parents were doing. They helped by gathering firewood
and brush branches for their beds. Children helped to carry
them home. Young as they were, they would all do it. Little

ones all helped to carry something over portages. Every little thing helps and they had little paddles and they loved to paddle.

Through doing all this they learn how to work, but in the beginning, it is play. Little girls learn how to make doll moccasins. The mothers would make a rag doll stuffed with moose hair and a wee papoose cradle board. Children started snowshoeing very young for they had to walk when parents had to travel.

When I had babies, I kept them in a papoose cradle. The cradles have three different sizes; small, medium and large. You would change the back board as the baby grew out of it. We used moss in place of diapers. Using moss on a baby is most healthy. The baby always smelled sweet and was always warm. We would change them every so often by discarding the damp moss and replacing it with some clean and fresh smelling. No washing to do, how nice!

We kept our babies in a papoose cradle for ten to fourteen months. Some might be walking and still in a papoose board. The board was made of cedar wood, because it is the lightest wood. The front bar is made out of maple wood as it won't break when bent. It also had a board at the feet for standing and a cloth or leather for lacing up the baby inside it. The babies seemed to like to be in a papoose cradle for they would cry to get in it. It was always very hard to break away from this cradle, but they can become too heavy to carry around.

We always prepared moss in the fall before the snow came. Expecting mothers would do this. The sphagnum moss was dug in swamp country where the cranberries are and cut into square blocks about fourteen inches square. A tree would be felled leaving the trunk and branches so that they would be visible in the winter and protected from being covered with snow. The blocks of moss would be placed on top. It takes about forty blocks to carry one through the winter supplies. As you needed it, you would bring one block into the house.

Moss has a lot of roots and, after you pull out all the roots, the moss is soft as cotton batting. If you don't stock up before snow falls you soon discover how hard it is to dig moss under snow, especially with the ground being frozen then too. This is what I mean when I say you have to study a lot of things about what to do ahead of time when living in the wilderness, off the land and nature, as we did in days gone by.

🐻 *The Burden expedition...*

IN 1928 WE WORKED IN THE MAKING OF A MOVIE called 'Silent Enemy:' a semi-documentary of the Indian way of life and their struggle to survive. This, one of the last silent films ever made, became known as the Burden Expedition. The producer was a man named Douglas Burden and he had some support from the Museum of Natural History. While one hundred local Indians took part in it, the two main Indian actresses came from the U.S.A. They did not even know how to put on a snowshoe and I had to teach them myself how to use them.

The hero of the movie, was Long Lance the noted personality from North Carolina. He stayed apart from us and we thought he was snobbish. It wasn't until later that I learned that he was not a real Indian but rather a black man, Sylvester Clark Long. Maybe he was afraid that we would learn his secret. The other main actor was Chauncey Yellow Robe from New York. He was friendly and a genuine native person. Other Indians came from different places, with four families coming from Bear Island: Mr. & Mrs. Alex Paul and family, Mr. & Mrs. John Turner and family, Mr. & Mrs. John Katt and family and our

Myself and Frank Broda, the Head cameraman. An unidentified cameraman on the left. Photo taken at Rabbit Chutes east of Temagami, in February, 1928.

The wrap up of the making of the Silent Enemy film in 1929, showing Head cameraman, Frank Broda.

Great Uncle John Katt with his family at Rabbit Chutes during filming of The Silent Enemy in 1928.

My husband Alex Mathias and New York Indian Actress Dorothy (Doe) Tomekin, at Rabbit Chutes in 1928.

family, my husband Alex, my brother Donald Petrant, my sister Lena Petrant and myself. Other Indians were from Timmins, Ontario, North Temiskaming, P.Q., and Mattawa, Ontario. Among those Indians were several papoose. All took part in the picture at one time or another. At first, every one settled down and lived close together in tents. It was like living in a little village with nice people.

We began the picture in September and ended it in April, 1929. The scenery was to be from the fall season through winter and spring. In the picture, we all wore full Indian costumes. But, from this group of Indians of about one hundred, only four women , one of them being me, knew how to work with

Dorothy (Doe) Tomekin, myself and Mollie Nelson posing for a photo during filming at Rabbit Chutes, 1928.

Long Lance wearing a wolfskin hat with Dorothy (Doe) Tomekin, during the making of the movie, The Silent Enemy, north of Temagami in 1928.

Mollie Nelson, an American Indian actress from New York during the making of The Silent Enemy.

the leather to make such items as moccasins and mitts, or how to fill the snowshoes. Anyway, every person had to have a full outfit, even the little ones. The Company furnished the hide for everything and raw hide for the snowshoes.

Don't think we four women weren't busy! Mrs. John Turner, Mrs. Alex Paul, Mrs. Annie McBride and myself, had to make one hundred complete Indian outfits in one month for use in the picture. This meant working all day and part of the night.

Father Eva, Jesuit Priest, with white beard (seated), Monseignor Dupius with fur hat (standing), during the 1927 Christmas gathering. The priests cashed the cheques of salaries made by area natives working in The Silent Enemy film. Once cheques were cashed donations could be made to the church. My cheque was in the amount of $60.00. I am well back in photo.

But, even with this extra work we women did not get more wages than the others. The two leads got a big salary and they never could do anything useful. Believe me, we worked hard to have everyone outfitted for the picture.

The men made snowshoe frames of all sizes. Even the little ones who could hardly walk had to have some for the picture. The men also made sleighs, toboggans, tepees, birch bark canoes and paddles as part of the setting.

The company took many pictures of our families, sometimes as individuals and in some parts, as a group in a village. One exciting part was when we shot the rapids. The cameramen set up their cameras at the foot of the rapids and five canoes went down the river with five people in each canoe. I was in one of them. It was beautiful to see this and I am sure it helped to make the picture interesting.

I also played the part of one of the three wives of Mr. Paul Benoit, playing a part in the movie. One wife was an elderly woman and she took part in hunting, to bring food for us to eat. I took part in cutting wood for heat in the tepee and working around the tepee preparing meals for all. The third wife was just a young girl and never did a thing except to be company for the husband while we other two wives worked like slaves for the husband. He never did a thing except loaf around with his young wife, like real lovers. We other two were to make life very comfortable for both of them. I waited on them hand and foot. We pretended to be very scared of him. What a laugh!

The picture was really a lot of fun to do, but not very authentic. When I think of some of the things they had us do, from dancing barefoot in the snow to carrying a bear cub in a canoe while shooting rapids, I really wonder. It's too bad they didn't pay more attention to us who knew better.

In this picture, they had a lot of things on the go. But some parts were really crazy. John Turner felt that too many things

Dorothy Tomekin (New York City Indian actress) and myself in 1928 at Rabbit Chutes camp, the filming site for The Silent Enemy. Dorothy didn't know how to put on snowshoes, so I had to teach her.

were cut out of the film. Maybe that was alright. The Company made their own rules about Indian way of life and we Indians had nothing to say. We just took our orders and went along with them as we were all getting a salary. Amazingly the film had some success and parts have been used recently by the National Film Board.

My husband, Alex, was not in the picture. He was a mailman for the Company. In the winter he used dog teams, and once the lake was open he used an outboard motor. Often he would travel from Rabbit Lake to Temagami Station and from Rabbit Lake to Kipawa. Usually he was out every day. Alex was well-liked by the Company, as he was a hard working man.

This film was shown at Cobalt and once in North Bay, but I was unable to see it either time. When the picture was shown in Cobalt, I just had given birth to my first baby, Dorothy. When the next time it was shown in North Bay, my baby, Virginia had just been born. So, I was out of luck both times, but I was disappointed. It would of been so interesting for me to have seen it myself. I never did see the whole production. Later I learned that this was one of the last silent films.

The Burden company also had a lot of live animals. These animals were used in the picture in some parts. They used such livestock as moose, deer, wolves, beaver, otter, black bear and wolverines. They also had a staff of thirty altogether. I know because I had to cook for them.

One morning at 4:00 a.m. their cook walked out on them and they asked me to take over until another cook could be found. I went and it took two weeks before a new cook appeared. Was I glad to see that woman come as this was my first experience cooking for the staff. One day, the manager came to me and said to me, "There is only one thing wrong with your work." Of course, I was very nervous and new at that work, but I replied, "Yes, what is it?" Said the man, "You cut your cream

American Indian actor, Chauncy Yellow Robe, one of the leads in The Silent Enemy *film.*

pies too small." Well, he sure scared me, for a minute I thought I had done something wrong. Anyway, they were all happy, but I wasn't for I was too anxious on the job. The new cook didn't come any too soon.

However, during the time the picture was being taken, we had a lot of fun by ourselves. We used to gather together in the evening and square dance and sing songs. Among the Indians were good violin players and good step-dancers too. We had a lot of enjoyment with a very nice group of people.

The picture was started at Kipawa River and after a few weeks, we moved up the river and settled at Rabbit Lake. Most of us spent the winter in a tent where we used wood stoves for heat. At Christmas, we had a lovely holiday. As most of the Indians were Catholic, a priest from Haileybury, Father Eva, O.M.I., visited us. He brought money so we could cash our cheques and give our Christmas donation to the church. We had a lovely Christmas mass. It was indeed beautiful. In April, we moved back to Kipawa River to finish the picture. When the picture ended, it was rather sad. We all left for home, everyone in a different direction. With the exception of those from Bear Island I have never seen those people since, from 1928 to the present.

🐻 Living with nature...

WHITE MAN MAKES A FARM to grow hay to feed his animals. He also grows vegetables for food. Indians also feed their animals, only in a different way. Around the middle of April, the Indian trapper looks around to find a bare spot, mostly up on the rocks where the snow goes first, where there is still a lot of snow at the bottom of the hill. They set a match to this bare spot and only burn where it is dry and bare, so there's no danger of a big forest fire because fire stops when it reaches snow.

Two years later you would find a big patch of blueberries in amongst the bushes. And you should see all the hungry animals of all kinds feeding on those blueberries; fox, wolves, black bears, partridge, squirrels, chipmunks, and all kinds of birds. No doubt those animals were happy to find those berries. It was the trapper that got it for them by setting the fire.

This is what I mean when I say Indians feed their animals too. The berries were for our own benefit too. As we would preserve them for our winter use. After a few years, young trees would grow on that burnt place. Then the rabbits would get to feed from those young bushes. In later years, the little trees would get bigger. Then the moose and deer get to feed from it. So, you see the setting of these small fires can go a long way in feeding many animals.

In the olden days there were no jars for preserving or canning fruits or berries. We used to dry the blueberries by spreading them on a big sheet of birch bark and letting them dry in the sun. When dried they are like currants and they keep. We also would cook down the blueberries till very thick and leave this in a cake form until dried hard. When needed, we would chip a piece off the brick and pour a little water and sugar on it. This would make a lovely preserve.

We also dried chokecherries. Chokecherries are very good as medicine. It is especially good for diarrhea, stopping it almost at once. We would put the chokecherries in a pan, pour hot water over them and drink as tea. The tree bark of the chokecherry tree serves the same purpose and is also good to heal sores. Over the years Indians have studied a great deal about medicines out of nature for many different kinds of illness. For us this was great because it did not cost anything but our hard work, at the same time this medicine made interesting learning.

I remember away back through the years, when I cured a little Indian girl. This little girl, about four years old, had been in a hospital for several months. Finally the doctor advised the mother of the child to take her little girl home as he had given up on her. The doctor said, "We cannot do anything more for her. Her life is a matter of time. The girl has tuberculosis in the bone. There is nothing we can do." Naturally, the mother was very upset. So I asked the mother if she would mind if I took over to see what I could do for her daughter. "Why, yes," said the mother and she showed me where the little girl had a running sore at the ankle joint.

I went home and looked for the beaver castor, as we always had some on hand. I soaked the castor in warm water to soften it. When it was ready, I took some over to their home. I put the beaver castor on the little girl's open sore and bandaged it up. Next day I changed the dressing. I did that every day for a whole week. It is unbelievable how much bad stuff had come out of that open sore, matter and blood both. Finally, it started to heal from the bottom of the wound. It was a very deep wound. By the end of one month the little girl was able to get around a bit and she had gained weight. Believe me, the mother was glad. In time the girl was completely cured. As I write, she is still alive, perhaps drawing her pension but still a picture of health, Mrs. Agnes Laundry of Temagami.

This beaver castor was so wonderful for so many different things in the way of medicine. We would always preserve some when we were trapping, to have it on hand when needed, it is also good when a woman is in labour. You put the beaver castor in a pan, pour hot water on it, strain it and drink it as tea. It works the same way as ether, with the same effect. Also, it is good for asthma. You soak the castor in gin and take the gin by teaspoonful as desired. It is also good for a sore tooth. The castor has a little cake of gum inside. So you take that piece of gum and insert it on a decayed tooth and it stops the pain. It is not a pleasant taste mind you, but good medicine.

🐻 *More memories from my early days...*

I REMEMBER IN THE OLD DAYS, we used to have a lot of snow through the winter, at least three feet or more. We used to blaze our trails and when the snow melted away, our blaze would be high up on the tree. In winter our house used to be very cold as soon as fire went out. When we got to bed the fire was always out shortly after. No fire until the morning. As I said before, my grandfather used to prepare the firewood at night. He always laid everything beside the stove to start a quick fire, such things as birch bark and small dry pieces of wood for a fast fire to warm up the house quickly. We always had a big wood pile in the house.

The log cabin was big to heat. All of us would use our rabbit skin blankets for warmth. This is when we had great benefit from these skins. The fur was so soft and warm that we never felt cold even when our water pail had about one or two inches of ice in the morning. Whenever this water pail was empty, we had to go to the lake and chop an ice-hole to get the water. Many a time our trail would be covered over by a snow drift. Whenever we lost our water-hole we would have to make another hole. Sometimes the ice was fourteen to sixteen inches thick.

In my young days, there was no school at my Indian village home. I had to educate myself. The little I know in English was

Paddling in Lake Temagami. In my early days everyone paddled, even the tourists.

learned through the Eaton's catalogue. I would look at the pictures and the names of the goods that were below the pictures. I studied hard that way. In later years, I met some English people and learned much from them. As time went by, I made a lot of English friends. Many of them helped me to talk English. Today I am still trying to better myself.

Right now I have decided to write the story of my life. I still find it difficult to put my words together and also to translate my Indian language and thoughts to English. Anyway, I try. It is all I can do. There is so much I would like to put on paper of Indian life, because I see it is a lost way of life. It is really a pity, because the young generation will never learn about it.

Very few real elder Indians are left that would know this Indian way of life. You can read a lot about it, but it is not always the truth, sort of a made-up story. I like to hear about the real facts.

My great-grandmother had told me a great deal of Indian life and it was most interesting to hear. But, I am not the writer that could get this all down on paper. I am better with my own life stories.

One of my own exciting experiences I remember, happened while trapping in the bush. One day my first husband and myself went out moose hunting. We came across a moose track. My husband said, "This moose track is fresh. He cannot be very far away." I replied, "How can you tell?" "Because the moose stool is not frozen yet," said Alex. So Alex asked me to stand still while he went after the moose. Sure enough, not long after he left, I heard a shot. Next thing I heard was my husband yelling at me, saying, "Beware, the moose is going your way!" I looked up and here was a terrible looking moose coming straight at me. He was ploughing through deep snow, his ears set back and tongue hanging down a foot. The first tree I saw I climbed up, snowshoes and all if you please. This was impossible to do, though I tried anyway, ha! ha! Anyway, the moose passed right by and never even saw me. At the first dead log it came to, the wounded moose laid against it. My husband came along. He only had one more bullet and he wanted to save it. So he got his axe out and chopped the moose's head off on that log. Well, we had moose to ourselves again and lots to eat.

In our days when we lived in the wilderness, it was so nice and quiet. Once in a while, you would hear some robins chirping and singing and you would hear them all answer one another. At night you could hear owls calling to one another. Sometimes you would hear a fox barking or wolves howling. At other times you could hear a beaver slapping its tail on the water, or a partridge drumming on a dead log.

I used to sneak up on a partridge while it was drumming and I would get close enough with a long pole with a snare wire at the end of the pole. I would reach the partridge, snare its head and jerk it. Then I would have my partridge.

We would also hear the falls running and frogs making their noises in a pond. I love to hear frogs. The wind blowing in the trees almost makes music when the branches and limbs are rubbing together. The air was fresh then and the water was pure. It was so wonderful to live with nature. Even with the hardship, it was special.

We have watched the North Star, our compass to guide us while in the woods. In the fall while we were trapping, wherever we were on the river or a lake, when the water froze up on us, we would just turn down our canoe and start walking towards home. Travel through the thick bush sometimes would take two to three days before we would make it home. Sometimes it was very hard walking with no trail to follow, just very thick bush, but it was always good to get home. All of these are wonderful memories.

Regatta Time at Bear Island. We were always there.

🐻 *The fisher was very scarce...*

IN MY TIME WHEN I WAS TRAPPING, the fur bearing animal called fisher was very scarce and was considered a most valuable fur. A family of trappers would perhaps only get one fisher a year, very seldom two a year. Therefore, whenever we came across a fisher track, all trappers did the same; track the fisher tracks. Follow it up until you could catch it. One never knows how long it will take. Sometimes it takes only two to three hours and other times, two to three days. Once you follow the track, it cannot be left because if snow comes, the track is covered and you lose it. So, you don't take chances.

On one of our travels, my husband, sister, brother and myself came across a fisher's track. At the time, we did not have much food with us. Anyway, we started to track this fisher, not know-ing how long it would take. We travelled until dark. Mind you, we did not go very far as the fisher certainly makes his trail crooked; up hill, down hill, around the hill, climbing up trees and jumping from one tree to another. Then we would have to try to find where he started walking again. Sometimes it would be several feet away and then sometimes we almost meet our-selves. But, this is the chance you take when you track a fisher.

Along the road we killed a partridge, cooked it and shared it among the four of us and drank the broth as tea. We did the same with rabbits. We would stop overnight by an open fire. We made a brush lean-to towards a cut rock with the fire at the rock to throw back the heat into our shelter. It kept us warm though through the night, but if it had snowed, it would have been a lost cause.

After two nights of staying out, we finally caught up with the fisher. My husband peeled birch bark and filled the hole where the fisher went in amongst the big rocks. Next, Alex gathered birch bark and set a match to it in the hole. As soon as the smoke got to the fisher, he came out right through the flames. First tree he saw, he climbed up to the top. My husband shot him. The fisher was a little singed on the fur, but not too bad. Sometimes, the fur gets very damaged and we lose the value of the fur, but this was a good catch for us.

The fisher were very scarce, today I do not know of the numbers.

🐻 *More hardships and tragedy...*

ANOTHER PARTICULAR TIME that I have never forgotten happened at the end of March when the going was rough with heavy snow. My husband, my oldest daughter, Dorothy, and myself came out from the bush. We had a dog team and the girl was on the dog sleigh. Alex and I walked on snowshoes. After walking a few miles, I asked my husband to stop and make a fire to make a pot of tea. Shortly after, we started again and made another few miles, when again I asked Alex to stop for another pot of tea and a little rest. We started off again and we just went a little way when I had to stop again. I was played out. Alex said, "If we stop so often, we will never get home." But, I was so tired as I was seven months pregnant at the time.

Anyway, we had a pot of tea and we still had two miles to go on the lake. I could see the point where our cabin was. I asked my husband, "Would you have a string on hand?" Yes", said

Alex and he handed over some string. I tied a string on one snowshoe and one to the other one. So there I was, every time I took a step, I lifted up my string to help me lift my snowshoe. I did that the rest of the way till I got home. Believe me, that was tough going.

That same spring my brother, Donald Petrant, was in the hospital and at the age of 24 he died of tuberculosis at the beginning of April, 1937. We went to his funeral at Bear Island and decided to stay there. On May 7th, I had my girl, Virginia Mathias. She was only three pounds at birth. Mind you, she was an eight month baby and I had no doctor. The travelling was so bad at that time as the lake was only partly open. This delayed the doctor in getting up to Bear Island in time. Anyway, the doctor told the mid-wife that the baby would not see the day out as she was so poorly. She was very delicate, but she lived and is still living. She is now in New Brunswick having had three healthy children.

She owes her health, too, to a hospital in Boston which treated her on a trip I made in 1938. If it hadn't been for that hospital, the baby would never have lived. The doctors did a wonderful job on her and she had special care. However the doctor there also told me if it hadn't been for the care that the baby got right after its birth, she would never have lived. How well I know the difficult times I had with her, day and night both. I certainly put in a lot of time and worry about her. Virginia is the only one living out of my three children.

At an earlier time, in 1933, when we lived in Diamond Lake, my husband and brother built a nice log cabin for ourselves. It was indeed a lovely home. It was in a lovely spot with flat rock and a nice sandy beach. There was a nice little bay where this house was situated. The logs were pine logs and the house had two large windows and a nice white wood floor. In the summer months, a dentist from Haileybury, Dr. Crawford, used to stay in it when he came to fish. He would say, "You could eat off the floor, the house was so clean." A big range was in the house and I used to bake eight loaves of bread at the time. It was a good stove. We had a table with benches to go with it and two home-made beds. In fact, everything was handmade, cupboards and all.

One day, lumbermen got into that area and cut logs. They spoiled this lovely good fishing lake by raising water to drive their logs out. When the water was raised our house went under

My grandfather Michel Katt Jr. shown with 3 of his grandchildren. Myself, brother Donald (died 1937), and sister Lena (died 1950). Photo circa 1930.

water with everything in it too. We lost everything and never got a thing for the loss of our home. The lumberman said the Hydro Electric Commission of Ontario held the right to store water on Lady Evelyn Lake and its tributaries of which Diamond Lake was one. We had to lose our home without compensation. Years later a letter released from the Hydro Commission in Cobalt said that we had no right to be on the flood plains. But we did not know that nor were we given any warning and never any compensation

🐻 *Other areas of work...*

THIS ONE YEAR WE DID NOT GO TRAPPING. We worked at a small silver mine, the Golden Rose Mine south of Temagami at Emerald Lake. There again my husband was a mailman. Alex would travel from the mine to Bear Island Hudson Bay Post and sometimes he had to take the boss to Temagami by outboard motor or by dog team in the winter. He had four dogs to a team.

Myself, I worked in the kitchen as a cookie. One day, a strange thing happened to me. In the store room everything was in big quantities. In one place I spotted a big bag of bran. I started making bran muffins and they went like hot cakes. Everyone like them, so I made more. One day the boss came into the kitchen with a teamster. The boss said, "Madeline, have you seen a bag of bran in here anywhere? The teamster has lost a bag of bran for his horses." I replied "Yes, there is a big bag of bran in the store room, but I have been using the bran for the muffins and the bag is nearly half gone. I am sorry." The boss answered, "That's all right, you can keep the bag. Those muffins

Alfred and Charlotte Horr from Cleveland (my Grandfather's first tourist retainer) at their summer camp. Husband Alex and myself looked after the lake camp for 13 years, summer and winter, until Alex died of 'TB'.

are delicious, so keep making them." Well, the teamster wasn't very pleased that I had robbed his horses. I too had had a funny feeling about using that bran, but I thought it was for our kitchen. Anyway, I used it in bread too and I baked lots of bread. With forty men working in the mine, I put out a lot of lunch boxes.

One day, I made the cook mad. He used to fry steaks and the poor fellows could not cut their meat, it was so tough. Finally, many would never even touch the meat. But, I did not like to see it wasted, so I put it on to boil for a long while, until tender and then I added salt pork, carrots, turnips, onions and thickened it and served it in big bowls. Did this stew ever go! Everything was cleaned up. So every time this cook would fry steaks, I would make the stew afterwards with the steaks that were not touched. One day the cook said to me, "Everyone in the camp is laughing at you." Why?" I asked. He said, "The men call you the 'Irish Stew Woman'." I replied, "Well they like it anyway and they always clean up everything." I finally quit my job as a

The regatta at Bear Island circa 1936. A popular time for tourists.

cookie. The cook was too hard to get along with. The boss was sorry to see me go, but my husband Alex stayed on till spring.

In the summertime, we had our regular job to go to. For thirteen years we worked for the same American tourists at Island 672, Lake Temagami. This private camp was opened in 1919, owned by Mr. Horr and Mr. Yenne of Cleveland, Ohio. There were many landowners from Cleveland, Ohio. One family we liked very much were Mr. and Mrs. R.B. Newcombe. Much later we were shocked to hear of a tragedy in their home. It was reported that Mr. Newcombe killed his wife, Faith with an axe and then committed suicide.

Three or four families of very nice people would come every summer to spend five or six weeks at the camp. My husband and my brother, Donald, were their guides. I used to bake bread, pick blueberries and bake blueberry pies. We would cook also a lot of fresh fish, as the tourists loved that.

When we worked for those people we used to open the camp for them. Every year my husband used to fill the ice-house. He would put in forty blocks of ice, each a 16 inch square block. He would saw the ice himself and use a dog team to carry the ice into the ice-house. He covered it with sawdust to last all summer long. This ice would keep meat and fish fresh. We would keep cold drinks there too. Every camp had an ice-house. It was a job for people to do to fill the ice house during the winter. The ice house is a thing of the past.

We spent thirteen wonderful years at that camp. It is still open in the summer months. A younger generation is now running it, but I remember all of this so well.

🐻 A play for the tourists...

I PREPARED A PLAY ONE TIME for the tourists, a very interesting experience for me. It was during the month of August in 1938 that this play about Indian life at Bear Island came about. At that time we were a group of about twenty Indians altogether.

To begin our little history of what took place, I will give you a brief summary of the Indian inhabitants who displayed their skills in the Indian way of life. They included: Chief Pishabo and Lucy Pishabo; Mr. and Mrs. Tommy McKenzie and their two children; Mrs. Whitebear; Mrs. Alex Paul; Mrs. Missabie; Mrs. John Twain and her papoose; Mrs. Donald McKenzie and her daughter Eva McKenzie; Mr. Joe Paul; Mrs. Maria Potts; Mrs. Enos Twain and her papoose; my daughters, Dorothy and Virginia and myself, Madeline Mathias.

Our setting consisted of one birch bark tepee, one brush lean-to, one brush wigwam, four baby hammocks and one open fire. In the performance, everyone who took part was fully dressed in costume. Chief Pishabo wearing feather head-dress, took care of the fees. He was supplied with a moose leather bag into which people dropped money, whatever amount they desired to give. Eva McKenzie, his little helper, rewarded the money-givers with a piece of moose leather as a souvenir to attach to their clothing.

Lucy Pishabo, wife of the Chief, interested the passers-by with her demonstration of smoking tanned moose hide over a pail with a smudge of dry, dead poplar wood. Tom McKenzie displayed bows and arrows along with his splendid carvings. Mrs. McKenzie assisted her husband by showing their little papoose in a cradle and displaying the moss which is used on ba-

89

bies in place of diapers. Little Adam McKenzie, who was about four years old, entertained spectators with his little bow and arrow and toy birch canoes.

Mrs. Whitebear aroused the curiosity of the on-lookers as she arranged the twine and demonstrated the making of fish nets about fifty feet long. Her efforts did produce a fine strong workable fish net. Mrs. Alex Paul's part of the demonstration was to fill in the centre of the snowshoes. Both she and I cut thin strips of raw hide, moose hide (bibeche) to be used for the snowshoes.

Mrs. Peter Missabie sat outside of her brush wigwam busily making birch bark baskets. From time to time Mrs. Missabie and myself, Madeline, would show people how to untangle a fish net and how to fold it into the proper position. Mrs. John Twain was busy in the open air working on moose hide. She had the hide hung up and would pound it with a big, wooden hammer. Then she would stretch it back and forth until dry. At the time her papoose was lying comfortably in the swing under a shady tree.

Mr. Joe Paul, with a 'crooked knife' and small axe, showed the tourists the art of making bow and arrows as he worked beneath the shade of a birch tree. A crooked knife is used to make snowshoes, bows and arrows, canoe slats and ribs. It's cutting edge is drawn toward the user. The blade has a curve at the end. The wooden handle is at an angle to the blade. He also made paddles out of maple wood. Mrs. Donald McKenzie was baking bannock (bread) over an open fire while Mrs. Enos Twain was cooking meat on several one-foot sticks and placing them around the open fire and gradually turning them around until the meat was thoroughly cooked.

Mrs. Tom Potts demonstrated the making of beaded moccasins and beaded bags. She also showed how to make a rabbit skin blanket by looping the strips of fur. Her papoose lay nearby in a swing beneath a shady birch tree.

Virginia Mathias, my daughter, who was fifteen months old

and still in a papoose cradle, caught the eye of tourists as she was such a pretty little girl with long black curls and big blue-greenish eyes. She was secure in her ornately beaded papoose cradle which stood against the birch bark tepee. Her arms were out and she played with her toys which hung down from the front bar of the cradle face rack. The toys were made of duck beaks, dried and laced together in a bunch. They make a tinkling noise when rubbed together. All the toys were made out of nature.

Dorothy Mathias, my oldest daughter, then eight years old, was dressed in full Indian costume. She played around the birch tepee with her little black pup.

Finally, the whole group of Indians seated themselves around

A gathering on Bear Island. Catherine (Whitebear) Missabie, Bessie Paul, Cecine (Whitebear) Baker, Helen Paul, Sophia (Missabie) Katt.

Mr. and Mrs. Alex Paul at Bear Island in their later years. He was the person in charge of burials when the priest was not there. He died at home on Bear Island, at age 104.

the open fire and ate the fresh bannock and meat which they had cooked. After the big feast of bannock and meat the group of Indians entertained the audience with a pow-wow dance.

The play was a lot of work, but was beautiful. Later I saw the movie picture made from it. It was most interesting to see, almost unbelievable. A Mr. Goddard, the owner of the Temagami Hotel, had taken shots of this play. There were individual close-ups of everything. I tried to borrow the film, but this man would not let me have it. He was the lucky one. It did not cost him a cent to get those pictures and he was able to make a movie out of it. It was a beautiful film for him, too.

Our misfortune, however, was that on the day we had the play it was very rough weather with high winds. Many people could not get across the lake to attend the play. Only a few people came, just those who were able to come on a big boat.

Anyway, the making of this play had a lot of planning put into it. The women made their own costumes, but I bought the material for them. As for the meat we demonstrated, I paid for that, and also for the night letter to the Sudbury Radio station to announce the play. I also paid the man who brought the poles and birch bark to make the tepee. With what money we made on the collection from the tourists, I paid off all what we owed. We ended up with one-fifty ($1.50) to the good. So we had $1.50 to share among the twenty of us in the play, but we had fun anyway, if nothing else.

The only one that really got the monetary benefit out of this play was Mr. Goddard, who took the pictures and made the film. I often wished I could have shown it to my friends. All of the costumes in the movie were beautiful. My papoose had a mass of bead work on the papoose cradle and she looked so pretty arranging those toys of duck beaks. Everything, even the articles on display were beautiful in the picture. The background was in the open at Bear Island, but with lovely trees all around.

I would give anything to see that picture again. Of course, by now most of the people who were in the play are now dead, perhaps two or three living out of the original twenty. To the best of my knowledge this film still exists. This historically important account should be available for the public record and for my people to enjoy.

🐻 *Dealing with hard times...*

SHORTLY AFTER ALEX MATHIAS AND I WERE MARRIED in 1923, the beaver season was closed by the Lands and Forests law in 1928. No reason was given. To this day I have never been given an explanation. From then on we looked after our trapping ground by raising a beaver park.

It is surprising how fast the beaver multiplies. It was so wonderful to see the park grow with beaver houses here and there on every little lake and beaver dams in all the rivers. It is known that beavers are great workers. In ten years this park of about thirty square miles was thick with beavers. Living in such an area you get to see the beautiful work that beavers do. Wherever you go there are beaver swimming or eating at the shore.

In 1937 the beaver season was re-opened. That very same year, much to my regret, my husband was sick at home at Bear Island, and was not able to trap.

In those days, Indians were not allowed to buy a trappers' licence, but as long as they stayed in their trapping grounds, everything was fine. However as soon as they leave, the next one that comes can claim it. So this is what has happened to our beaver park. We lost it because my husband was sick and couldn't go to our trapping grounds. Other Bear Island trappers took over and killed off all beavers. They made thousands of dollars on that park. We never got a cent out of it and we could have used the money too. All our care of this park was for nothing. After the hunting ban, times had changed. There was no more sharing.

My husband was ill for three years. He suffered from tuberculosis. What a tough time we had! At the beginning of his illness,

A publicity shot from the 1938 New York City Sportsman's Show. At left is John Turner of Bear Island. Next is an unidentified American who had worked for Mr. Burden during the making of The Silent Enemy film. I am beside another Native from Quebec dressed for the show. We were one week in New York followed by one week in Boston. I staffed the booth and answered questions about artifacts on display.

we received twenty dollars a month for four of us in the house. This was called a ration from Indian Affairs. Well, it just wasn't enough. So I used to skin trappers' game such as beaver, mink, fox and fisher. I would trade my work for food to help along our twenty dollar ration.

To heat our house, I had to sell some of our furniture. We would trade it for fire wood. First I gave both my canoes for wood, then our boat and engine next. We had four guns that went for wood too. After three years, our house was empty. Each time we were short of wood, I would give something, my table, chairs and cupboards all went. When my husband died, all I had left was two beds and a stove. Besides all of this, while I was sitting up at nights with my husband, I did a lot of knitting of socks and I sold them for food.

Anyway, in 1937 at the beginning of my husband's illness, I had obtained a job for one month to work for a Sportsman Show. This was to be two weeks in Boston and two weeks in New York. My salary was to be two hundred dollars plus my train fare of sixty dollars.

My boss, John Turner, a Bear Island entrepreneur, still had contacts with New York as a result of the movie made in Temagami in 1928. He said, "I will take my wife with me, so you could come with us in a car and bring your family with you. You can give me that sixty dollars you got for fare to pay towards the gas."

In February 1938, we all left for Boston. At that time my baby Virginia was nine months old. Alex looked after Dorothy, seven years old at the time, while I worked at the show. I had

FACING PAGE *A camp demonstration at Cleveland YMCA promotion in the fall of 1929. Photographs of this sort were sold to the public.*

With daughter, Dorothy at their Bear Island house built by husband Alex. Photo taken shortly before his death in 1940.

Virginia in a papoose cradle and she was to be in the show with me. On my first day demonstrating native customs at the Sportsman Show, the baby cried and someone reported us. So our boss said, "I have to take you and the baby to the children's hospital." When the doctor examined the baby, he found out that she was troubled with mastoid in the ear and that she had rickets and pneumonia. The doctor suggested leaving the baby in the hospital. I did not know a soul in Boston and was so upset. Believe me, it was heartbreaking to leave my baby behind, but I just had to do it.

Through the night we had a call from the hospital saying I had to go and give blood to the baby because she was too weak to fight the case. John Turner took me to the hospital to give my blood to baby Mathias. From then on the baby improved, but I had to leave her there for nineteen days.

Two weeks later we left for New York. I left Virginia behind. This was not easy. The doctor said he would get in touch, which he did, to inform me of the baby's condition. I was so grateful to him.

We spent two weeks in New York at the Sportsman Show. Each place we were at, we got a light housekeeping apartment and we bought our own groceries. It was cheaper that way for Alex and myself. When we finished our work in New York, we went back to Boston to pick up Virginia.

I paid the hospital and the doctors and came home to Bear Island. When we got home we had one dollar and fifty cents left to the good from the two hundred and sixty dollars I had made. But, I had my baby on the mend. I would have lost her if I had stayed at Bear Island because the doctors at Haileybury did not know Virginia's troubles. I had had three doctors see her and none of them knew what her illness was. So thanks to my trip to Boston and the doctors there for my daughter's health and her life today.

Anyway, I was not worried coming back home broke, as I figured I had money coming to us at the Hudson Bay store and also another month's ration coming due. Altogether I thought we had forty dollars available to us.

As we arrived home, I went to the store to shop and asked for our ration. The Hudson Bay manager replied, "Sorry, you have nothing coming to you." What a blow that was! I asked, "Why?" The manager said, "Well, you were making money and you do not need that help." This was much to my surprise. I did not know what to do next. Anyway I said to the manager, "I can not understand that." "Well," said the manager, "the Priest was here to stop it for you because you are working making money."

I went home and wrote a note to Indian Affairs at Sturgeon Falls. In the meantime we had nothing in the house to eat and the baby was crying from hunger. Later a Mrs. Angele Turner came in and seemed to make fun of us because we were so sad. But she went straight to Mrs. John Turner, her sister-in-law, to tell her. Mrs. Turner was shocked at the news. At once, she went to the store-room at their hotel and filled two hamper baskets with groceries. She and her daughter delivered it to us by canoe.

Mrs. Turner said to Alex, "Why did you let this happen? You should have come to me for help and I would of been more

Display at the 1938 Boston Sportsman's Show. One of the promotional photo's sold to visitors.

than glad to help you." She gave my husband six dollars to buy a case of milk for the baby himself, – "You buy it because," said Mrs. Turner, "I don't know what brand of milk the baby takes. Do buy it yourselves." This kept us until we had settled this money problem with Indian Affairs and we received further notice about our ration.

A few days later Father Wittic received the letter I had written to the Indian Affairs, as it was sent back to him. Well, he was mad. He informed me that I would have to go to North Bay to the Bishop, where he would charge me for talking about a priest. "I have your own hand-writing in black and white to show the Bishop, so you haven't a chance," said Father. I replied, "I will. I will do anything for my own child." Well, I never heard any more about this. The next news I received, the Hudson Bay store manager asked me to go over and see him. When I arrived there he suggested I pick up the supply of groceries I needed. That was indeed a happy moment.

However, shortly after that we were isolated because of the tuberculosis. We could not go anywhere and the girls had to stay right in their yard. It was really tough for several months before my husband's death. On March 6, 1940, Alex died. My oldest daughter was nine years old and the baby girl was nearly three years old.

🐻 *My ordeal with tuberculosis...*

RIGHT AFTER MY HUSBAND'S DEATH IN 1940, Dr. Arnold of Haileybury sent us to have x-rays. We went by dog team to Temagami and then by train to the Haileybury Misericordia Hospital operated by the Sisters of the Assumption. The children were alright, but I was in very bad shape and needed hospital care. The doctor asked the Sister to book me into the hospital. Sister, refusing to take me, replied to the doctor, "Her husband was to come here and he never showed up, so we are not taking her." They held that against me.

Dr. Arnold suggested that my two daughters be taken away from me. They returned the same day to stay with their great-grandfather at Bear Island until something could be done for them. Later, they were placed in a boarding school at Spanish, Ontario.

I had to leave the hospital and returned by train to Temagami where I stayed with Mrs. Whitebear for one month, as I had no where else to go in my condition.

By May when the weather was warmer, I returned to Bear Island to my almost bare house, by myself. There were only two beds. Finally, I was bedridden and could not get up any more. I was weak by daylight and slept when it was dark because I could not light my lamp. Some days, someone would come in to bring ready-cooked food and leave it in my plate. I never knew when the next one would come. People were afraid of me, but I did not blame them as tuberculosis was considered to be contagious.

Father O'Neill, the replacement for Father Wittic, used to come in once in awhile. He would say, "Don't give up, Madeline, I am trying hard to get you in the hospital. Be patient." I have seen the day when it was so hot and I was so thirsty for water. The pail of water was at the table, but I could not get to it for a drink. Only when someone came in, did I have my thirst quenched. I was so very thin and weak that I never never thought I would come out of that illness.

Finally, five months later, on October 10, 1940, Father O'Neill came in and said, "I have good news for you, Madeline." He had a letter with him which he read to me. It said,

'*You take that lady to the hospital and if the Sister turns her down again, let me know at once. I will take the matter up at the parliament building this time.*' It was from Mr. Walter Little, the Mayor of Kirkland Lake. He was the only person who offered to help Father O'Neill get hospital admittance even though he had requested assistance from several sources. Father O'Neill said, "I will take you up tomorrow morning, so get ready for nine o'clock."

My great-aunt, Jessie Dennis, came to help me to get dressed and Father O'Neill picked me up with his boat and took us across to Temagami Station. He put me in his car and drove to the same hospital in Haileybury. As we arrived at the hospital, Father asked the Sister for a chair to put me down and he showed her the letter. Right away she said "Oh, yes, we have a bed for her." One of the nurses took me up to the room. Was I pleased! I cannot put it in words to tell you how happy I was to get into a hospital.

I did not see Father O'Neill any more until a week later. He came to visit me and he asked me how I was. I replied, "Fine, I am so happy I am here so I will not die all by myself." Father O'Neill answered in a very angry manner. He said, "Madeline, do you love your children?" I thought it was a funny thing to be asked for I was the mother. I replied, "Yes, Father." Father said, "You certainly don't sound like it. You have two beautiful girls and they have just lost their father and they need you now more than ever. Therefore you have to be a mother and a father both and I brought you here to get better and here you are, you want to die." He was mad. "By dying, you are not going to help your children," said Father. Anyway, as he was leaving for home, he said to me, "I will be back in a month's time and when I do, I want to see you looking better."

After Father left, I felt very sad. I got thinking about what Father had said. The children did need me. Well, from then on I fought back to get my health again. I made myself eat and sleep a lot to regain my strength.

One month went by before the Father visited me again. He was glad to see me, because I had improved a great deal since he last saw me. After twenty-six months in the Sanatorium wing, I came out cured at Christmas time 1941. I have never had a set-back to this day. I had good doctors who couldn't do enough for me. Through their care, I was turned into a new person. While I had a lot of treatments in the hospital, it is thanks to the good Lord and doctors that I am here today.

When I left the hospital, the government paid our room and board for six months in advance to give me a head start. After that I was on my own. Once more I had my daughter Virginia with me, now four and a half years old. Dorothy was still at boarding school.

At this time I started living white man's culture when we were placed at a home of a nurse.

 *My new life...*

AT THE START OF A NEW YEAR, 1942 and a new life, I was living and working in a Nurse's home. She informed me that since she worked at the hospital she had her meals there. I was to give her husband his breakfast, lunch and supper at home. I was to put butter at his plate for toast. "But you and Virginia eat lard on toast," said the nurse. We went along with that. And we never saw sugar either. Finally my little girl cried because she wanted sugar on her corn flakes, but there was never any sugar around for us.

One day we were out for a walk along the road. All of a sudden a car drove up to us and stopped. Here was our Dr. Arnold from the sanatorium. He asked how we were doing. I said,

"Fine, except Virginia misses her sugar. She cries when she eats dry corn flakes." The doctor replied, "Don't you have your sugar ration book?" I said, "No, I don't know anything about a ration book." Dr. Arnold answered, "You should have your book and Virginia should have her own book too. Ask the nurse for it, she must have it."

When the nurse came home, I said to her, "The doctor told me to ask you for the ration books." She looked in her bag and threw the books on the table in anger. She said, "What do you need them for?" The next day I went to the store with those books and I asked for sugar. The manager said, "Sorry, lady, there is nothing here for the next two weeks. All the coupons are pulled off." Well, we had to wait for another two weeks before we could get sugar.

I used to make doll moccasins and sell them to buy sugar for ourselves. We had no money even though the nurse got paid for our room and board. Yet how I worked hard at this place!

One day the Nurse brought home three patients. Those patients were not sick enough to hold a bed at the hospital and they were not well enough to go home to their Indian Village. The hospital needed their beds. One man was stone blind, one had heart trouble and the other fellow had epileptic fits. The blind man had a running sore between his ribs. The nurse was supposed to look after his dressings, but she never did. I changed it for him every day.

I don't know how I ever managed to do all the work I had to do. I did all the laundry for seven people. There was no washing machine and I washed in the bath tub with a washboard. I knelt down to scrub the clothes and I hung them outdoors. I did all the cooking and served their meals. Some days, they had visitors. One day I had fourteen people to serve.

That same afternoon after I finished my dishes, my little girl and myself went for a walk. It was a beautiful Sunday afternoon.

While walking on the road, a car drove up beside us. Again here was Dr. Arnold himself and again he asked how we were. "All right, but very tired," I said. "Why?" asked the doctor. I replied, "I had fourteen for dinner, because the nurse had visitors." The doctor was upset. He said, "This won't do. They are getting paid for your room and board. You don't have to work like this." Anyway, he decided to move me away from there and he found another place for me.

This new place was better. But there was still a lot of work there as the woman was rather sickly and had three girls going to school. Her husband, Jim Anderson, was a guard at the Haileybury District jail. Anyway, the work did not hurt me. We had good meals and all we wanted to eat. We were very happy there with very nice people. The husband gave me one of his old uniforms and I made it over and turned it into a woman's suit. It made me a lovely tailored suit.

After six months my room and board was no longer paid by Indian Affairs and I had to support myself. I left this place to room out and work out by the day. Both girls had gone back to boarding school at Spanish. On Wednesdays I used to work for Dr. Arnold's wife. One day Dr. Arnold himself asked me if I would work for him at his office. I didn't know anything about office work, but the doctor said he would teach me how and tell me what to do. His assistant was getting married and he wanted me to take her place. So, I did. I would go in to work at 1:00 p.m. and finish at 6:00 p.m.

Shortly after Mrs. Arnold asked me to live in with them in their home. She suggested that she would give me room and board and I would do the morning work for her and the office work in the afternoon.

I took the offer. The house work was heavy: on Monday mornings I did the washing, at noon the dishes and from 1:00 p.m. to 6:00 p.m. the office. After supper, there were more

Me in the uniform I wore while working for Dr. Clifford Arnold, M.D. in Haileybury. Dorothy and Virginia were in boarding school at the time.

dishes to wash and I baby-sat the rest of the evening. Tuesday mornings I did the ironing and the rest of the day was repeated from the day before. Wednesdays was general cleaning in the office, the clinic and the sitting room. On Thursday the morning was general cleaning all through the house and from noon repeat again the afternoon work. Friday morning, I washed the clinic linen and again I repeated the afternoon work. Saturday, once more the same work. Many days I put in fourteen to fifteen hours a day.

This was my introduction to the white man's way of life.

🐻 *A second marriage...*

MY LABOUR FOR THE DOCTOR and his wife ended when I married Arthur Theriault, in January 1946, a second marriage for me. I met him in December 1945, through his sister Annie while I was working for Dr. Arnold. He had a son Edwin, three years old at the time. We made our home in Haileybury. This time I worked at the jail for awhile as matron. Eventually we bought a house with a lovely garden on Albert Street. We had so much space in our lot; three apple trees, many red plum trees, a big bush of raspberries, blackcurrants, gooseberries and nine hills of rhubarb. I had enough rhubarb to supply the whole of Haileybury. We had one plot alone where we just planted potatoes. I sold some as there was too much for us.

I hardly saw any summer for I was too busy with our produce. I made jelly with apples and mixed fruit jelly, that was especially good. Every kind of fruit from my garden was preserved; apples, plums, raspberries, gooseberries, black currents and rhubarb. Much was given away. I also canned a lot of wax beans, peas, and tomatoes. I pickled beets, made beet relish, and lots of nine-day sweet pickles. They were especially good. This was a lot of work, but it was a good living. It was so great to be able to grow your own food.

Every year I was short of sealers for preserving and I kept buying more. One year, I kept count of how many jars of food I gave away in one year. Altogether there were ninety jars, mind you, ninety jars of fruits of all kind, pickles and preserves, both jellies and jams. These experiences show what I mean when I say I have lived in two cultures, both the Indian way and white-man's way. It is all work mind you, but great living in both ways, both very interesting. My second marriage gave me another home and a chance to work again and be with my family.

Unfortunately this marriage did not have a happy ending. After ten years we parted and went our separate ways.

Arthur Theriault, Dorothy, myself, Virginia, Edwin (Arthur's son) at Haileybury in 1946, the first year of our marriage.

Virginia, at age 17, wearing a new dress I made for her. Photographed at Haileybury in 1954.

🐻 A new type of career...

WHEN I REMARRIED THE FRENCH MAN I lost all my Indian rights. At this time my oldest girl was fifteen and the younger girl was nine years old. While they were both at boarding school at Spanish, it was necessary for me to earn some money..

110

Before the girls came home in the summer holidays, I worked at the jail in Haileybury as matron. I was on night-duty. It was my job to lock up the female inmates for the night and remain on guard duty until morning. It was hard for me to keep awake all night since I did not read. One night as I was going on duty, I took a bunch of old rags with me, and after I had put the prison girls to bed and locked them up in their cells, I started cutting these rags and braiding them. I sewed them together and in no time I had a rug made. So, from that time on in 1946, I made rugs and until just recently I continued to make them.

Since that time up to this day, I have made in the neighbour-hood of a thousand rugs in all shapes, sizes and colours. Most of those rugs are made out of used material. Any material goes into it as long as it will braid. But there is a tremendous amount of cutting of rags to make that number of rugs. I was very fortu-nate in that many of my friends helped me to gather old cloth-ing to make rugs. It takes a lot for one rug alone. Some I have sold for wedding or shower gifts. I sold three rugs to buy a dress for my late sister Lena to be buried in. This was one time, I was very glad I had those rugs, as I did not have the means to buy the dress.

Another time when I remember it was handy to have a rug to sell was when Virginia was going to school at St. Joseph's Col-lege, North Bay. I wanted to visit her and we had a car to travel in at that time. I asked my husband to take me as we were living in Haileybury then. My husband replied, "I have no gas." So, I called the garage. A lady answered and I asked her if she would be interested in buying a rug. "Yes I would," said the lady, "but I have no money right now." I replied, "I am not asking for money, I want gas." "Well," said the lady, "bring your car, I will gladly fill it for you." So we drove the car to this garage and the lady filled the car full. I gave her two lovely braided rugs and she was so happy. So was I. We went to North Bay with great pleas-

Virginia Mathias in the Canadian airforce. 1957.

ure after all to visit my daughter. She was glad to see us as she was very lonesome there.

Those rugs have done me many a good turn. Making braided rugs continued as my hobby. I really was able to get along well in this world in some strange ways and I am very grateful for that. Those rugs I have made are now all over the country and in the United States too.

When I lived in Haileybury, I did a lot of sewing and alterations. I made children's clothing and turned coats into outfits for little children. Also I would sew men's pants into boy's pants and men's suits into women's suits. I also made lovely skirts from men's pants.

One day, I was at a Catholic Women's League meeting as I was a member. A parish priest attended the meeting. He gave us a talk and said, "The Bishop is going to send our wardrobe to the missionary, so we have to buy our own vestments and we need five sets. To buy one, will cost us three hundred dollars." Of course, I opened my big mouth and I said, "Father, wouldn't it be cheaper to have it made? How much would it cost to get the material alone?" Father replied, "I will ask Sister she should know." Sure enough Sister came and figured it all out. She said, "Sixty dollars complete." Well, then Father asked, "Who would make it?" Some of the ladies said "Mrs. Theriault can, she spoke about it." I replied, "I have never made anything like that, so I couldn't." Sister said, "That's no problem, we will give you one set to go by." So, I had to give in and I said, "I'll try."

The Sister ordered the material and she asked me if I would make it in the basement of the church and make one set first to see if I would succeed. Father said, "Make one and if you do all right, you can make the others." I replied, "I could not sew in the basement." "Why?" asked Sister. I said, "I have a baby at home, my grandson, whose mother had died not long ago." The Sister said," Bring him over with you." I said, "No, it is much too cold here for a baby." Anyway Sister replied, "Well then, I will go over to see your place first before I bring the material, because it is valuable and I wouldn't want it to get marked."

She came to see my house and she found the baby, Donald, was securely in a corner and all round him were his toys. Anyway, I made the vestment, a black set, and displayed it at the card party. It was approved and I did not charge for the first one, but did for the next four sets, white satin, purple, green and red, I got paid $20.00 in total or $5.00 a set. Believe me that was a lot of hand-sewing! Everything was lined with silk and was hard to handle. There were five pieces to each set, the vestment, restband, long stole, purse and a cover for the chalice. By making the five sets I saved the church one thousand dollars.

When my second husband left, I moved to North Bay with my two grandchildren. At the beginning it was rather tough. I pressed charges against my husband for non-support, but he did not do anything for me. So, my doctor put me on welfare. That was hard. I had my two grandchildren to raise. I couldn't work much, only now and then as I was troubled with arthritis. The girl was seven years old and the boy was five years old. Finally, I got help from the Red Cross and they did a lot for us. The Imperial Order of the Daughters of the Empire (I.O.D.E.) also gave us used clothing and I would make them over for the children to wear to school. The Kiwanis club gave us milk for several years and we received Christmas Cheer packages. However,

This 1959 photo shows me with daughter Virginia, in her airforce uniform at Saint John, N.B. in 1959 with Dorothy's children, Gloria age 12 and Donald age 10. I raised the youngsters after Dorothy died in a fire in 1950.

I am glad I moved to North Bay. My grandchildren have been educated and now both are doing well and living in North Bay.

I have a lot to be thankful for. So many have been kind to us, but at many times it was mighty tough going. In ten years, we moved from one place to another twelve different times because we couldn't pay the high rent. But, despite all we worked hard to survive.

Now that the children are on their own, my thoughts are always thankful for our having made our way through. One of the most difficult times was when my oldest daughter was a victim of fire and left her two children behind. Those are the grandchildren I raised myself. That was a very sad time and very hard to face. But I never lost faith and never gave up.

🐻 *My reflections as a senior...*

At present, I am in my 80's and living in a Senior Citizen's building. I am very comfortable, happy and contented. Until just recently, I have been very active and a member of many clubs - the Catholic Women's League, the Civic Hospital Auxiliary, the Indian Friendship Club, the Senior Citizen Club 70 and the Golden Age Club. I attended those clubs whenever possible. It was always interesting to see and belong to groups and be part of what was happening. I still love to meet people too and have friends all over.

I am most happy to be able to get out when I can and I really believe I am very lucky to be alive after all that I have gone through. I was in the sanatorium for twenty-six months and came out of it cured. I had a goitre operation and I have lost one eye, I broke my arm and I am still going strong. Until my failing eyesight prevented me, I did a lot of knitting of socks and mitts and the crocheting of hats. I have made a number of patchwork quilts and many, many braided rugs.

I also did much travelling. I have been to Cleveland, Boston, New York, Florida, Nashville, Tennessee, Wheeling, West Virginia, Niagara Falls several times, St. Catharines, Kitchener, Kingston, Toronto, Mississauga, Sault Ste. Marie, Agawa Canyon, Gaspé, P.Q., Montreal several times, Ottawa, Midland, Parry Sound, Cobalt and Haileybury. For me all of these trips were most enjoyable with beautiful scenery. I fully enjoyed all of it!!!

I hope I have expressed myself clearly in this write-up. It was very difficult to translate Indian words into English as many Indian words are part of living off the land and nature. I spoke Ojibway only for all my early years. It wasn't until I was about 16 years of age that I began to learn English words. Alex had learned some English as a result of the time he lived with Archie Belaney, later known as Grey Owl.

In my time, there was not much schooling, just four months a year and you only could go up to Grade Five. An Indian Affairs representative said that was the highest school of all, and we believed him for the longest time. Anyway, I regret to say I did not go to school at all. My great-grandmother was very old and she needed looking after. So, my grandfather wanted me to watch her. She smoked a pipe and we were afraid she might set fire to herself. She was also stone deaf. Grandpa thought it was more important for me to watch over her than go to school. Anyhow, the Indian children did not learn much during four months of schooling.

By the way, all the difficult times I had with the white people did not make me condemn them. I just figured I had to face whatever came along and accept how we were going to be used by white man. I made no fuss about it for the longest time, I just took it all. Little did I know there were some good people in this world besides those who put me down and kept me low through so much of the time. We always came last in the eyes of so many.

Indeed there are a lot of fine people who are true, kind and so willing with helping hands. For instance, the lady doctor, Dr. Stewart, I had when I was in the sanatorium in 1940, is someone I kept in tough with until her recent death. She had been a real true friend. She was very nice to me and you couldn't have asked for a better person in your life. This doctor did so much for me during my illness and brought me back to health again with God's help. This, I shall never forget.

So, my life has been fulfilled many a time over with true kindness and love. I have been well liked in many ways by many kind people! Of course, I have run into some unthinking people through time. For example, this one instance, I have never forgotten or really got over. My daughter, Virginia, was sick one day and I took her to Dr. Arnold. While seated at the doctor's office, the

Living today in North Bay.

doctor asked Virginia, "What grade are you in?" "Grade thirteen," said Virginia. "What do you want to be when you finish school?" asked the doctor. Virginia's reply was "practise law". The doctor laughed out loud and said, "What makes you think you could become a lawyer, Virginia? Did you ever hear of an Indian lawyer, Indian doctor or an Indian Priest? Never!" said the doctor. Poor Virginia, her heart dropped and from that day on Virginia lost interest in school. I felt badly because I had backed her for thirteen years and encouraged her.

From then on I could only help her by looking after the home, by making it comfortable for her and making clothes for her school so she could have all the time at school to study, which she did. The teachers told me she was a good student. But, after that visit to the doctor, Virginia's hard work and hard studying fell flat at that moment. It was really a shame as she was doing so well. Anyhow, in later years, Virginia took up book-keeping and typing and worked out till she raised her family. But that unfortunate experience showed what expectations we could have towards education.

When I was living in Haileybury, I was a member of the Catholic Women's League and did the work of a social worker. I would go to the hospital and visit twenty-five patients at the Incurable Ward. My grandchildren were with me then. Donald was around four and Gloria was six years old. I used to dress them up and take them with me when I visited. It was such a treat for those patients to see small children in their ward, as no children ever went to them. Donald was a talkable kid. He chatted away with them. It made the patients, their hearts, good to see children and I was glad to make them happy.

I used to get $7.00 a month from the Catholic Women's League to treat these twenty-five patients. Out of that I would take cookies and candies or cigarettes for those who would rather smoke. Anyway, to make my treats go farther, I used to bake cookies and make fudge and mixed it with the others, so the parcels would be bigger. The patients would look forward to my coming. I was told they missed me so much after I left for North Bay.

When I came to North Bay, I visited the sick for two years in both hospitals for the Golden Age Club. Then I had to quit. At that time, there was no bus, so I would walk to both hospitals. This was rather tough going and more than I could manage.

But, later when I moved into the Edgewater Apartments in 1981, I had many activities going on, such as card parties, shuffleboard, darts and several other games. Besides that, I would attend meetings of my clubs and take in their tours. Along with the work I had to do at home, and my handwork, I kept busy.

About fifty years back, all Indians had Indian names. My late husband, Alex, was known as Ke ji pe ta ke ji ko o ne ne. It means 'fast day man'. Mine is Ka kita wa pa no kwe. It means 'wise-day woman'. My oldest daughter's Indian name, Ne pe te wa pa no kwe, means 'one-by-one day woman'. It doesn't rhyme the same in English as in Indian words.

Well, today, in my new quarters, my biggest amusement is my tape recorder. The children gave it to me for one Christmas some years ago and I get so much good out of it. I tape songs I like, and many of my friends' voices. I sometimes tape myself in the Indian language, or tell Indian stories. This is one way I can hear Indian words. It is nice to hear the Indian language, a language which I never hear any more. It is a pity it is lost. So, I get much enjoyment from my tape recorder, the children couldn't have given me anything better. My family are very good to me and I have a lot to be thankful for and feel so richly blessed.

From 1973 to 1980, I made hundreds of braided rugs or mats as I have mentioned. At the Edgewater Apartments alone I gave away close to 200 mats as gifts. Most of the apartments have mats I made. People in that building were wonderful. Many would save old clothing for rug use, and help me gather the material needed for mats. I felt part of the life in that building.

In my years there I saw a lot of changes, such as people moving out, people getting married, others going to nursing homes and some dying. We have lost many nice friends, but we must carry on and love the ones left behind. There is much we can do for one another.

I love all people and I like to make everyone happy, because it makes me happy too. God bless us all!

Madeline Katt Theriault